# BLACK MARKET

## INSIDE THE ENDANGERED SPECIES TRADE IN ASIA

GLOBAL CRIME SYNDICATES PROFIT FROM A NEW CONTRABAND

# BLACK MARKET

## INSIDE THE ENDANGERED SPECIES TRADE IN ASIA

Ben Davies

*Introduction By* Jane Goodall

*Produced by* Adam Oswell / *Main photography by* Patrick Brown

EARTH AWARE EDITIONS

To the brave men and women who
risk their lives to conserve some of
the world's most endangered animals.
That their efforts are not in vain.

**EARTH AWARE EDITIONS**

17 Paul Drive
San Rafael, CA 94903
www.earthawareeditions.com
info@earthawareeditions.com

Part of the proceeds from this book will be used to
develop further awareness of this critical issue facing
Asia's wildlife. This fund raising activity is supported by
Earth Aware (www.earthaware.net) and Palace Press
International (www.palacepress.com).

We ask your assistance in distributing Black Market
worldwide through your network of individuals
and organizations. Please contact
blackmarket@earthaware.org with any questions about
how you or your organization can get involved.

Produced by Adam Oswell
in cooperation with Earth Aware Editions

Library of Congress Cataloging-in-Publication
Data available.

ISBN 1-932771-22-0

10 9 8 7 6 5 4 3 2 1

Designed by Insight Design

Executive Editor: Raoul Goff
Associate Editor: Jim Pollard
Photo Editor: Roland Neveu
Managing Editor: Lisa Fitzpatrick
Production Manager: Usana Shadday
Design and Layout: Ian Szymkowiak & Alan Hebel

Manufactured in China
by Palace Press International—www.palacepress.com

# CONTENTS

# Wildlife Trafficking Regions

RUSSIAN FAR EAST

GUANGZHOU, CHINA

HUKAUNG VALLEY., BURMA

PABITORA-KAZIRANGA NP
ASSAM INDIA

MONG LA, BURMA

VERAVAL, INDIA

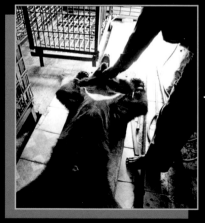

HANOI, VIETNAM

BANGKOK, THAILAND

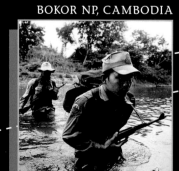

BOKOR NP, CAMBODIA

MEDAN, INDONESIA

PHNOM PENH, CAMBODIA

# INTRODUCTION

## By Jane Goodall

*Black Market: Inside the Endangered Species Trade in Asia* is an extraordinarily thorough investigation into the wildlife trade throughout Asia. Author Ben Davies and producer Adam Oswell have travelled widely, visiting Australia, Burma, Cambodia, China, India, Indonesia, Laos, Malaysia, Nepal, Thailand and Vietnam. The facts uncovered are deeply disturbing, laying out in great detail the horrific capture and slaughter of millions of wild animals. While many people are dimly aware of this holocaust, very few outside the conservation community—even within it—realize the magnitude of the disaster. The author describes in graphic detail how wildlife is being plundered and trafficked from the once pristine jungles of Cambodia (for years protected because the Khmer Rouge made it unsafe for poachers), Vietnam, Indonesia, the great national parks of India and Nepal, and almost all other areas where some wilderness remains.

Ben Davies has researched the history behind the proliferation of wildlife killing in parts of Asia, such as the Chinese cultural beliefs that perpetuate its rampant consumption of animals. He covers the despicable practice of bear farming in Vietnam and China; the smuggling of ivory and rhino horn in India, Asia and Africa; and the shocking exotic live animal markets of Burma and Indonesia, especially the sale of protected birds. The book describes the huge problems faced by those working in anti-poaching patrols and the courage of so many of the men and women involved. The investigation into the organized criminal syndicates involved in large scale trafficking of endangered wildlife is chilling, just as the information regarding key individuals desperately fighting this major global crisis is inspiring.

It is essential to understand that, for many people around the world, the parts of certain animals have traditionally been thought to have almost magical properties. Some Chinese, for example, believe that they will gain some of the strength and power of a tiger by eating its flesh—just as some Africans believe they will benefit in the same way if they eat a chimpanzee. Bears suffer horribly from the conviction that their bile is medicinal. They are sold alive, forced into unbelievably cramped cages and the bile is "milked" from an often improperly implanted catheter. Some animal parts are thought to act as powerful aphrodisiacs, such as a tiger's penis, a shark's fin or a rhino's horn. Although scientific studies have shown that this is not the case, ignorance or mistrust of science prevails and the demand continues.

This book discusses the complexity of these issues throughout Asia. It examines the frightening size of the Chinese demand for wild animals and their body parts, and its cultural influence throughout the region. One wildlife conservationist in Cambodia likened the Chinese market to "a giant vacuum cleaner sucking out all the animals" in his own and neighboring countries. But the blame cannot be laid only on China. The smuggling of exotic birds and other animals, including fish and reptiles into Europe and America for the pet trade is a highly profitable business for dealers in many Asian countries, though the hunters seldom see much of the profit. The bush meat trade, the commercial hunting of wild animals for food, has also grown out of all proportion worldwide.

It is just too easy, in many parts of the world, to engage in the international trade in wildlife. The estimated numbers of creatures involved is staggering: thus 25,000 to 30,000 primates, 2 to 5 million birds, 10 million reptile skins (and many live reptiles) and more than 500 million tropical fish are exported each year. How much longer can population remain viable in the face of this relentless exploitation? If something is not done, and done soon with the determination and backing of key organizations in the international community, hundreds of species of endangered wild animals will be pushed to the very brink of extinction. Some will become extinct. Others will be moved onto the endangered list. Thus it is desperately important for the developed nations to step in and support wildlife conservation in Asia, to help both national institutions and non-governmental organizations working on the ground. Often these organizations need not only money, but also help in the planning and management of their conservation programmes.

We must remember that it is not only the illegal wildlife trade that is pushing hundreds of wild animal species towards extinction. They also face habitat destruction as human population grows, as forests are exploited for timber or charcoal, as wet lands are drained and developed, as rivers are dammed and overused for agricultural irrigation, as deserts spread in the wake of deforestation, over grazing and soil erosion. And, of course, wild animals are hunted for food by local villagers, as they have been for centuries.

Unfortunately, in most developing countries, issues related to the environment and wildlife come low down on the political agenda. Instead the focus is on crippling poverty, disease, surging population growth, and lack of education, not to mention civil unrest, armed conflict and terrorism. It is not surprising that government officials in charge of wildlife are typically underfunded and often have but little power. By contrast, those dealing in the illegal, international, multi-million dollar wildlife trade are making huge amounts of money—including many people in very influential positions. As a result, attempts to bring poachers and dealers to justice often fail from lack of funding and lack of support or even hostile opposition from superiors. Many of those with jobs in wildlife enforcement agenciest more or less give up and sink into apathy. And those who do care and who make determined efforts to control the trafficking, often lose their jobs—sometimes their lives—for "overzealous" attempts to incriminate influential wildlife smugglers.

The problems seem insurmountable. But there is hope. The author describes programmes designed to wean poachers and villagers off long term dependence on wildlife by introducing alternative ways of making a living. We at the Jane Goodall Institute have developed such community-based conservation programmes in several parts of Africa, with encouraging results. *Black Market*, by increasing awareness and understanding of the trade, its size, the problems involved in combating it, and the catastrophic consequences that will result if it is nor curtailed, will hopefully encourage governmental and public support for the many excellent conservation programmes of this sort that already exist, and the initiation of new ones.

The author believes that "It is in Asia's schools that the battle [to control the wildlife trade] will eventually be lost or won" and describes some of the educational programmes that have been introduced to Asian children. It is, of course, necessary to ensure that government officials and the general public are aware of the facts. But it is especially important to educate children. This is an aspect of conservation to which I am presently devoting most of my energy. What is the point of any of us working desperately to save wildlife and the wilderness if, at the same time, we are not educating new generations to be better stewards than we have been?

The Jane Goodall Institute has an educational and humanitarian program, Roots & Shoots, that is now active in more than 80 countries. It encourages young people from pre-school through university—and adults too—to make the world around them a better place by helping animals, helping the environment, and helping their own human community. Once young people understand the problems and are empowered to act, they can, and are, accomplishing great things. As I read the pages of *Black Market*, I was seized with a sense of urgency, for I believe Roots & Shoots could make a difference in this region, as it has wherever it has been introduced. So far it has only taken off in a few Asian countries—but China is one of them. We have already seen how it is helping to change attitudes towards animals and the environment there.

It is my firm belief that an understanding of animals as individuals can play an important role in shaping the way people think about wildlife. For it is not only the threat to a species that matters; so too does the suffering of individual animals. When I hear about the decimation of a chimpanzee population, I think about the living beings who are being killed or who are losing their homes. Each one, after all, has a personality as vivid and distinct as those whose lives I have observed for over 40 years—Flo, Fifi, Melissa, Gremlin, Frodo, and all the others. And this perspective is shared by many others.

Fang Ming read a Chinese translation of *In the Shadow of Man* when he was twelve years old, and it changed the way he thought about animals. "I never thought they could have personalities and feelings," he told me. He lives in Cang Nan County, Zhejiang Province, where the people traditionally eat wild animals. He decided to go out into the country and see how they were caught—and was horrified by the cruelty. He went back on several occasions to take photos, even though he was threatened. And then he went to record the cruelty in the markets. He showed these photos at school, as well as to his parents and their friends. Many people were shocked. In 2000, aged seventeen, he started the Green Eyes Roots & Shoots, with groups in four schools. They are very active, organizing trips into the country and educating the local people. They held a Bird Awareness Week at the County People's Square—Cangan County's first ever big environmental protection event. Several of the boys now brave the danger of following poachers and have given the local forestry officials information leading to the arrest of animal traders. When he was seventeen years old Fang Ming came to a Roots & Shoots festival in Beijing, and gave two major TV interviews. His passion, as he spoke, sometimes with tears pouring down his face, must have influenced thousands of viewers—and he has only just started. There are other young Chinese, Taiwanese and Japanese members who are just as committed, just as passionate.

It is just as important for a child in the U.S. or Europe to realize the consequences of buying an exotic bird from Indonesia or a *shahtoosh* shawl from China as it is to try to provide alternative ways of making a living to the Indonesian bird hunters and traders or those engaged in killing the Tibetan antelopes for their fine hair. For so long as there is a market, so long as people are prepared to pay high prices for illegal goods, human beings will find ways to continue their business and evade the law. Thus it is vital to educate those on both sides of the trade, the suppliers and the buyers.

*Black Market* is not simply a book of facts—although there are plenty of them, lending authenticity to the narrative. It is a book about real people, and real situations, often from the personal experience of the author. It is beautifully written in elegant prose imbued with a sense of urgency and drama that make each page fascinating and encourages one to continue reading to the end, despite the often grim and discouraging subject matter. It should be in every library, on the shelves of all Education as well as Environment Ministries, and it should be made compulsory reading for high school and university students both in Asia and the countries in the developed world that illegally bring in hundreds of Asia's exploited animals.

On behalf of the animals, thank you Adam and Ben for bringing their plight so poignantly and clearly into the open. Now it is up to each one of us to do our bit, in whatever way we can, to help.

*Jane Goodall Ph.D., DBE*
Founder, The Jane Goodall Institute & UN Messenger of Peace
www.janegoodall.org

# PLUNDER OF THE WILD

# WILDLIFE WARS

On a cliff overlooking the southwest plains of Cambodia, there is a bullet-ridden casino. The casino was built in the 1920s when Bokor was a breezy hill resort used by wealthy French colonials. During the 1970s and 1980s, it became the front line in the battle between the Khmer Rouge and government forces. But these days, a different war is going on.

It's night time and six heavily armed men make their way through the forest and tangled undergrowth using only the light of the moon. Carrying automatic weapons, they tread carefully stopping to check for animal tracks or to listen for signs of human activity. Up ahead they see a movement. One man signals and the others melt on either side of the track taking ambush positions. Gripping his gun, Ek Phirun, head of the unit shouts a command. A spotlight blazes, freezing the figure of a poacher. Surrounded and outgunned, the man surrenders without a struggle. This time the catch is small—a hog badger that will sell for less than US $20 in the local markets. But like so many species in Cambodia, it is endangered, with a price tag that could increase many fold, by the time it is transported further afield.

The poacher is taken away for questioning and later released. An off-duty soldier, he was simply foraging for wild animals to feed his family and supplement his paltry wages.

For the six-man wildlife patrol unit, however, the mission is deadly serious. They are trying to protect one of the last refuges of some of the world's most endangered species. On occasion, they have been fired upon or held at gunpoint. In one incident, several men received shrapnel wounds when a grenade was lobbed at them from the jungle. Separated from their families for long periods of time and often suffering from malaria, they are unsung heroes whose efforts go largely unreported.

Hours later, shots ring out further ahead, echoing through the wooded slopes and twisting pathways now swallowed up in darkness. This time the poachers are too far away for the rangers to pinpoint. Stringing up hammocks between the trees, the rangers sleep under the stars. The following morning they return to base in the village of Prich Nhil, their mission accomplished. "We can't stop the illegal wildlife trade, but we can make it more difficult," says Mark Bowman, a burly, six-foot-two military advisor for WildAid, a conservation organization that is helping to fund and train the rangers in a bid to save Southeast Asia's rapidly vanishing wildlife.

After thirty years of conflict, Cambodia is at peace. But when the fighting and the bloodshed

**Bokor National Park Cambodia January, 2003**

*A poacher being photographed and questioned by Cambodian National Forestry Rangers. The poacher has his name, age, the nature and date of his crime written on a board around his neck. He is from a four member poaching team.*

◁ Poachers are now using anti-personnel mines not only to disable their prey but also to deter forest rangers from destroying their traps.

# Like the illegal trade in drugs, it is demand from unscrupulous buyers around the world that fuels this grisly trade.

**Bokor National Park**
**Cambodia**
**January, 2003**

ended, the plunder began. Here in the remote national parks and forests, formerly controlled by roving bands of Khmer Rouge soldiers, everything has value. From the yellow vine that sells for a few dollars per kilo, to snakes, wild pigs, and even the innocuous centipede, poor villagers can supplement their wages by filling a few sacks with the bounties of nature. It's the prospect of big money, however, that is attracting the organized gangs of poachers who roam the countryside brazenly killing rare animals to supply the burgeoning international black market.

Like the illegal trade in drugs, it is demand from unscrupulous buyers around the world that fuels this grisly trade. As neighboring countries have exhausted their own valuable natural resources, the price for Cambodia's last population of tigers, elephants, and bears has soared to levels undreamed of even a decade ago. Killing a tiger can earn a poacher up to US $500 if he is lucky. With the average annual salary at US $200 and the price of a machine gun less than US $100, it's not hard to see why villagers become killers.

The laws of supply and demand have also led to a vicious circle. The rarer the wildlife, the higher the price. And the higher the price, the bigger the incentive for poachers to hunt down some

Unregulated trade is now the second greatest threat to ▷ wildlife populations after habitat destruction, while the illegal wildlife trade is the third biggest revenue earner for the international black market preceded only by drugs and arms.

# Now tigers and elephants are so rare that even the elite hunters who pay informers to spot these valuable animals

of the last great mammals on earth using anything from guns and snares to grenades and land mines baited with dead monkeys.

Months earlier, two elephants—one male and one female—were machine-gunned to death in the Cardamom Mountains in Cambodia's remote southwest region. The poachers hacked off the tusks, trunks, and bull's penis. Then they placed wire snares around the carcasses to form a lethal trap commonly used for catching tigers. Normally the poachers return at weekly intervals to check the traps in the hope of catching a tiger—an animal that is worth more dead than alive. On this occasion, the poachers stayed away, probably tipped off by the same guards who were sent here to arrest them.

When the killing is over the results are almost always the same. The most valuable wildlife is transported to a cluster of nearby towns and villages where local dealers temporarily warehouse it before they sell it to regional traders in the capital Phnom Penh. From there, it will be smuggled over the border to neighboring countries like Vietnam, Laos, or Thailand. The bones and parts will be used for traditional Chinese medicine, a system that dates back thousands of

**are finding it hard to locate them. As the big mammals disappear from the forests, so hunters are forced to turn to smaller and smaller animals to make their money.**

**Bokor National Park
Cambodia
January, 2003**

*A group of men from the Cambodian National Forestry Department cook their breakfast and prepare for the day ahead, reviewing maps of the area they will be patrolling.*

**Bokor National Park
Cambodia
January, 2003**

*WildAid law enforcement advisor
Mark Bowman, keeps an eye out
while eating his breakfast in the
Bokor forest.*

**Cardamom National Park
Cambodia
January, 2003**

*A boat from the National Cambodian
Forestry Department approaches
another boat with the intention of
searching it for poached wildlife.
The forestry department is checking
for wildlife being transported out of
the nearby park. Koh Kong, a border
village, acts as a major transit route for
wildlife being trafficked to and from
Thailand and Cambodia.*

years and is popular throughout east and southeast Asia. The meat will be eaten as a tonic, an aphrodisiac or an expensive local delicacy, while the skins will be sent as trophies to wealthy collectors in Asia and the West.

Mostly it's off-duty military or the police who are involved with illegal logging and animal trafficking. They provide high-level protection or lend poachers their guns. Sometimes it is local bandits or former members of the Khmer Rouge who have powerful vested interests in the trade. Either way the country's largest forested areas are being emptied of their wildlife.

The damage wreaked upon the forests and great mammals of Cambodia is incalculable. In the past five years, Sun Hean, deputy head of the poorly resourced Forestry Protection Department believes that 200 tigers have been killed, representing as much as 50 percent of the country's entire population. Now tigers and elephants are so rare that even the elite hunters who pay informers to spot these valuable animals are finding it hard to locate them. As the big mammals disappear from the forests, so hunters are forced to turn to smaller and smaller animals to make their money. If left unchecked, eventually there will be nothing left.

Cambodia is just one of many countries whose wildlife is up for grabs thanks to the endemic poverty of its own people and the insatiable greed of consumers and middlemen as far away as London, Beijing, and New York. Many of Asia's last virgin forests and wildlife strongholds are being plundered to supply the illegal trade—estimated by Interpol to be worth at least US $6 billion

Shooting is the most common method of poaching rhinos. In 1995 the first recorded incident involving a silencer was reported. Now, poachers also use either pit traps or electrocution of the animals by the dangling of wires connected to high tension power lines across rhino paths.

per year—and identified by police as one of the fastest growing areas of international crime.

The battle to save the region's wildlife, however, extends far beyond these remote hills and rainforests. It is being fought in Asia's schools and villages, where growing numbers of local communities learn the importance of protecting their environment. Increasingly it is also being fought at the international level where governments are under pressure to halt the trade in endangered species before it is too late.

The demand for change is coming from an extraordinary movement of people. Across the developed and developing world, men and women are coming together to make a stand. Their disparate ranks include celebrities, international environmental groups, local conservationists and concerned individuals who share one simple goal: to save what is left of their natural heritage.

The stakes are high. Tourists come to Asia in search of jungles and exotic animals. They expect to find a tropical paradise filled with elephants, dashing horn bills, and giant lizards. Unless action is taken now to stop the illegal trade, they will eventually find a dust bowl, emptied of its forests and its animals.

**Bokor National Park
Cambodia
2002**

*Cambodian National Forestry Rangers arrest a poacher during a night patrol near the village of Pichnil. Patrols in National Parks and protected areas in Cambodia are conducted as military exercises and can be extremely dangerous. Poachers are often heavily armed and malaria is common.*

**Bokor National Park
Cambodia
January, 2003**

*A poacher is moved by a member of the National Cambodian Forestry Department to an area away from the rest of his team for questioning. These teams are often commissioned to supply wildlife to larger traders and middlemen.*

# ...the poachers stayed away, probably tipped off by the same guards who were sent here to arrest them.

**Bokor National Park
Cambodia
2003**

*Cambodian National Forestry
Rangers during a law enforcement
training conducted by WildAid.*

FOLLOWING PAGE
*A team from the National
Cambodian Forestry Department
patrolling in Bokor National Park.*

Back on the rugged slopes of Bokor National Park, it's late afternoon and the rangers are already preparing their spartan rations for another five-day patrol, this time to the remote northern reaches of the wildlife sanctuary. These men can take heart from the 1,500-odd poachers that have been intercepted in recent times and the hundreds of animals that have been released back into the wild. But they are also the first to admit that it will take a lot more time and money before wildlife populations bounce back in many other parts of the region.

"Cambodia is still rich in habitat and wildlife. There is still a lot to save. But without fair and effective enforcement, there will be nothing left to conserve," says Jake Brunner at Conservation International, one of a handful of major environmental groups that have invested in conservation programs around the region.

Unless we act now to stop the illegal trade, we will eventually find only a dust bowl, emptied of all its forests and animals.

# THE EUROPEAN CONNECTION

Every thirty seconds, a plane takes off or lands at Heathrow, the world's busiest international airport. The staggering volume of traffic has made the London air-hub a natural target for criminal syndicates that want to fly in anything from drugs to cigarettes, or any other item of contraband. With more than 64 million passengers and 80 million bags passing through its four cavernous terminals every year, few of them get caught.

On a warm July morning, Charles Mackay, head of the Wildlife Customs Unit for Her Majesty's Government is called to inspect a shipment en route from Nigeria to South Korea. Inside a wooden crate tied up with rope he discovers ten rare African dwarf crocodiles together with a dozen royal pythons and a large collection of monitor lizards. Documents accompanying the shipment claim that the reptiles are legitimate exports bred on a farm in Benin. But vigilant customs officers recognize that the documents are fake and confiscate the consignment. Taped at the mouths and bent double inside sacks, the big surprise is that the animals are all still alive.

The crocodiles are taken to Heathrow's animal holding center where they are x-rayed for drugs. Police in Miami once discovered 39 kilos of cocaine hidden inside 225 live boa constrictors. The cocaine had been placed inside condoms and the snake's anuses sewn up. These days, customs in Britain take no chances. The x-rays reveal no illegal substances, only giant fishhooks caught in the back of the crocodiles' throats, which if not removed will eventually kill them. Veterinary surgeons carefully extract the hooks. The surviving crocodiles are then placed in one of the wire mesh cages that line the center.

Like the thousands of reptiles, birds of prey, and other wretched creatures that flood through Britain's ports every year hidden in specially perforated boxes, plastic tubes, or false-bottomed suitcases, the crocodiles were probably destined to become exotic pets for a wealthy private collector. "Had it not been for some inconsistencies in the paperwork, we would probably have never picked them up," says Mackay, a customs officer for almost thirty years. "The trafficking of high-value commodities is generally carried out with a very high level of sophistication."

*An example of a rhino bust.*

In 1996, police raided a lock-up garage in the plush London suburb of Kensington and recovered 120 complete rhino horns—representing the world's largest ever seizure. A 61-year-old man who was serving a life sentence for murdering his wife was conducting the sale of the horns from his cell.
▽

**London, England
September, 2003**

*Inside Scotland Yard's animal protection unit, a cabinet of items seized at Heathrow airport.*

**Scotland Yard
London, England
September, 2003**

*Inside Scotland Yard's animal
protection unit, an officer
displays a tiger's head seized
during a raid in London.*

"We get people
with poisonous
frogs, parrots,
reptiles and bear
skulls. You name
it, we get it."

– *Charles Mackay,
British wildlife customs officer.*

Never before has it been so easy or profitable to trade in wild animals thanks to better transportation and communication links and the opening up of even the most far flung corners of the globe. Every year, at least 25,000 primates, from 2 to 3 million birds, 10 million reptile skins and more than 500 million tropical fish are bought and sold around the world. And that's just the legal trade. The illegal smuggling of wildlife is believed to trail only the black market trade in drugs and arms.

Driving this seemingly bottomless appetite for rare and exotic species is a bizarre new phenomenon. Gone are the days when it was fashionable to have a chihuahua or a hamster as a pet. Today's fad-conscious owners want birds, snakes, and reptiles that are exotic to look at and easy to keep. For the truly endangered species, money is no object. On one occasion, Mackay busted a gang smuggling rare bird eggs into Britain in specially adapted underwear. On another, two live cheetahs. "We get tortoises on a regular basis," he says. "We get people with poisonous frogs, parrots, reptiles, and bear skulls. You name it, we get it."

Once the consignments get through customs, the wildlife is easily delivered to private collectors, zoos, or dealers who communicate by mobile phone and pay with cash, leaving little trail of their involvement. Wealthy buyers rarely get their hands dirty. If they do get busted, penalties for wildlife trafficking are in most cases almost laughable. "The big wildlife operators are virtually untouchable," says Mackay. "In their own countries these people have government contacts and they pay bribes. It is always the small guys that get caught."

It's a one hour drive from Heathrow Airport to the nineteen-storied glass-fronted headquarters of London's Metropolitan Police, which is situated a short distance from Britain's Houses of Parliament. It is here that the enforcement unit charged with monitoring wildlife crimes in the UK capital is based. But despite its grandiose sounding name, the resources allocated to the Wildlife Crimes Unit are pitiful. While the Metropolitan Police employs 40,000 officers—making it the biggest employer in London—it allocates just two full-time officers to the Wildlife Crime Unit, with four officers available on written request.

"The wildlife trade in Britain is not a priority for the Metropolitan Police," admits Andy Fisher, who heads up the department and has been instrumental in efforts to raise awareness

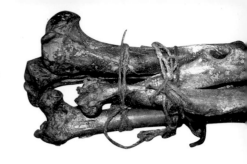

In 2003, 41% of 27 traditional Chinese medicine ▷
shops surveyed in New York City claimed to carry
products containing tiger bone.

about the illicit trade. "Fighting class-A drugs, theft, and anti-social behavior is where the Met concentrates its resources."

In his second-floor office, surrounded by posters warning against wildlife crimes, Fisher has a collection of animals and parts that almost any rogue dealer would be proud of. Thrusting his hands into a cupboard, he brings out a mounted ten-day-old tiger cub worth around US $6,000 that officers seized from a North London taxidermist shop named Get Stuffed. Fisher has shawls made of fleece from the endangered Tibetan antelope that sell for as much as US $17,000 apiece. Added to that are dozens of remedies containing tiger bone, bear gall bladder, and powdered rhino horn, confiscated from some of the hundreds of traditional Chinese medicine shops that have sprouted up around the capital.

Nowadays, to avoid the more stringent searches carried out in British ports, bigger wildlife shipments are frequently sent through neighboring countries like Holland, Belgium, Spain, and Germany. Once inside the European Union, illegal shipments can be moved across borders as easily as a truckload of vegetables. In January 2003, Hungarian customs officers discovered 2,700 dead birds hidden in coffins in the back of an Italian truck waiting to cross the Hungarian-Romanian border. Officers found the birds after a routine security check. Confiscations such as this, however, are as rare as many of the animals. It is no surprise that with profits as high as 800 percent and a low risk of detection, the illegal trade in wildlife is attracting the attention of more organized criminals.

But the tragedy runs far deeper, as men like Fisher are only too painfully aware. The failure of comparatively well-to-do Western nations to stop the illegal trade in wildlife has encouraged open slaughter of animals in the developing nations of Asia and elsewhere across the globe. Unprecedented rates of killing are in turn driving many of the world's rarest animals to the brink of extinction. "Elephants and rhinos are dying in Asia because there are people in places like London who have the money to buy them," says Fisher. "To beat the traffickers, we need a joint effort from both consumer markets and supply markets. At present, that is not happening." 🐘

In February 1997, British police seized 138 shawls made from shatoosh in the heart of London's Mayfair. It was estimated that up to 1,000 animals had been illegally killed to make the shawls worth £353,000 (US $473,000).

Since 1996, HM Customs and Excise have confiscated 1 million wildlife items at ports throughout Britain—equivalent to 570 wildlife items every day.

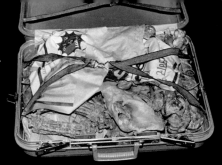

Powdered tiger humerus bone (for ▷
treating ulcers rheumatism and typhoid)
can sell for up to US $1,450 in Seoul.

# The Wildlife Trafficker

Lompoc Federal Corrections Institution is a low-security jail, situated north of Santa Barbara in the U.S. State of California. It is place where convicted criminals, drug offenders, and petty thieves wile away their days under the gaze of the prison's 173-member staff and where the biggest hope of inmates is the dream of release.

For 2 years and 329 days, Lompoc jail was the home of Keng Liang Anson Wong, the man dubbed Asia's biggest wildlife trafficker. Charged with forty counts of felony, wildlife smuggling, and money laundering, he was the biggest catch in the five-year undercover probe known as Operation Chameleon conducted by special agents from the U.S. Fish and Wildlife Service, the U.S. Customs Service, and Interpol.

To the people who knew him, Wong was the quintessential Asian businessman. Young and wealthy with impeccable connections, he ran a reptile park called the Sungai Rusa Wildlife Park on the tropical island of Penang off the coast of Malaysia. His was one of hundreds of privately owned zoos that have sprung up all over Asia in recent years. It stocked everything from crocodiles and snakes to rare tortoises and monitor lizards.

His park provided the wealthy Malaysian with a perfect front for his illicit smuggling operation. Wong would fly to the biggest international reptile fairs where he would purchase protected animals for his zoo. The only problem was that many of them never made it to Penang. Instead they were sold to other dealers on the international market, who sold them to wealthy collectors at fantastically marked-up prices. A large number of reptiles were smuggled into the U.S. concealed in express delivery packages, airline baggage, or large commercial shipments of legally declared animals. They included the Komodo dragon, the world's largest lizard, which can fetch up to US $30,000 on the black market and the false gavial, an endangered crocodile worth at least US $5,000.

What Wong did not know was that undercover agents working for the U.S. government were tailing him. For more than two years they had monitored his every move. They took details of the reptiles that he bought and sold; they negotiated to buy priceless and highly endangered tortoises from him; they recorded his phone conversations with dealers in Arizona and San Francisco. But the officers had a problem. Until Wong stepped foot in a country that had an extradition treaty with the U.S., they were not in a position to arrest him. So they arranged a trap, luring him to Acapulco. The moment Wong stepped off a plane in Mexico City, he was arrested and imprisoned on charges of money laundering and wildlife smuggling. He was eventually extradited to the U.S.

At a court appearance in California on 13 December 2000, Wong pleaded guilty to the trafficking of protected reptiles worth more than US $500,000 on the black market. He was sentenced to seventy-one months in jail and was fined a total of US $60,000. To all appearances it was one of the most successful undercover operations ever conducted by the U.S. Fish and Wildlife Service and a lesson to other traffickers of endangered wildlife species.

Wong, however, may have the last laugh. The reptile park that he owned still operates in Penang. On 8 November 2003 Wong was released from jail and extradited to Malaysia, where he is now a free man.

# BANGKOK Slaughterhouse

**The house stank of urine and feces. Flies buzzed over mounds of hacked off animal limbs and flesh, which were piled up neatly in crates on the floor. Picking their way through the carnage, even the most hardened members of Thailand's forestry police were shocked by what they saw. In one corner, a freezer was filled with twenty freshly cut bear paws. In another, the head of a fully-grown tiger was still attached to its skin. The body had been cut into quarters and placed in a cooler to ensure that the meat remained fresh.**

The tip-off, like so many others, had come through a network of local informants. When the vehicle carrying the first team of police arrived at this secluded farmhouse in Nonthaburi shortly before midnight, there was no sign of activity. The men surveyed the only entrance to the rambling old building until early morning before finally moving in. It was 8:00 a.m. on 28 October 2003.

Once the initial shock had abated, the scale of the operation finally hit home. The killing had been carried out with professional rectitude. The tiger had been shot at close range with a single bullet to the head. The bears had their paws cut off while they were still alive in their cages. Turtles, snakes, and dead pangolins were scattered around the house, ready to be transported to illegal wildlife restaurants like bags of fruit in a supermarket. It was, said police captain Aroon Promphan, a scene unthinkable in any civilized country.

In the back of the house, overlooking a secluded orchard where mango trees provide a shady awning, there were other surprises. Close to a dozen live animals waited inside steel cages for the inevitable slaughter. There were six live tigers as well as five bears and two baby orangutans. The only thing missing from the house was Leuthai Tiewcharoen, the owner. A notorious wildlife trafficker who had

**Wildlife Bust
Nonthaburi
Bangkok, Thailand
October, 2003**

*Police inspecting the remains.*

## Wildlife Bust

*Thanit Palusuwan of the Wildlife Protection Division Royal Forest department and Thai police inspect the slaughtered bodies of tigers, bears and leopards after an early morning raid on a compound in the outskirts of Bangkok. The raid represented one of the largest seizures of endangered wildlife in Thailand. The slaughterhouse was part of a high level syndicate with links in China and neighboring countries.*

The tiger had been shot at close range with a single bullet to the head. The bears had their paws cut off while they were still alive in their cages.

been arrested on two previous occasions, he fled the scene several hours before the operation took place. The sting did, however, successfully net two animal keepers along with a cache of weapons. So swift had the operation been that when police entered the compound, the men were taken by complete surprise. All that they knew was that some of the bears and tigers had been smuggled from Burma and that the meat was destined for restaurants around the country where it would be served to wealthy Thais and foreign tourists with a taste for the exotic. The two keepers were arrested and charged under the forestry and wildlife act. If found guilty, they face a maximum fine of B40,000 (US $1,000) or up to a year in jail.

Fortunately, where there are criminals there are also heroes; men like Sawaek Pinsinchai, the 58-year-old police major general, who was appointed head of the Thai forestry police only weeks before the raid. Soft-spoken and steely eyed with short cropped graying hair, he exudes a quiet determination that is consistent with his name—which literally translates as "servant of the royal court."

"I am not frightened of taking on wildlife traffickers," he says. "We are using the law and I have the support of the Prime Minister, the public, and the Queen of Thailand."

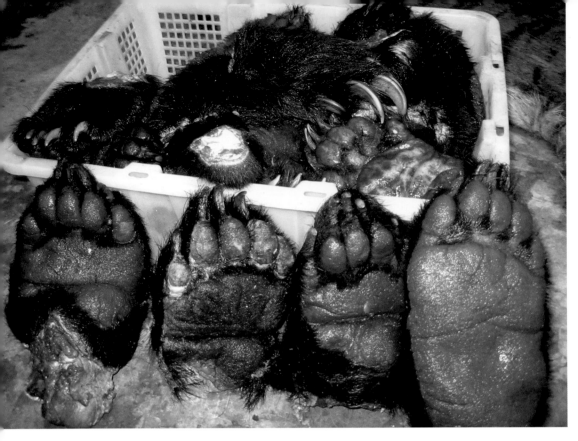

In the days and weeks that followed, the pieces of the jigsaw began to fit together. Sawaek's investigations revealed that the illegal slaughterhouse was just one part of a ruthless black market ring that also sent live animals over the border to Laos, Vietnam, and China. The operation had been able to flourish as a result of high-level protection. "This was one of the biggest and most powerful syndicates operating here in Thailand," he says. "From politicians to high-ranking officials and police, many people were involved."

But there was worse to come. Sawaek's investigations also revealed that the syndicate dealt in *ya ba*, an illegal amphetamine manufactured in Burma and sold throughout the region with disastrous effects on local populations. The previous year, a brutal crackdown against the drug trade had led to numerous deaths and uncovered the scale of the drug trafficking networks that operated with virtual impunity. As a result, the big syndicates were switching to alternative activities. With profits as high as *ya ba* and penalties so low, the attractions of the wildlife trade could hardly be greater.

The Nonthaburi raid, launched as part of a high-profile campaign against the illegal wildlife trade, was not the last. In a second spectacular raid conducted less than a week later, a team of over 300 police and forestry officials descended on Chatuchak, Bangkok's famous weekend market, seizing more than 1,000 protected species valued at around B50 million (US $1.2 million) and arresting several people. Among the confiscations were turtles, snakes, slow lorises, and hornbills, stolen from the country's supposedly protected national parks.

Bear paws that are used in a soup are considered a delicacy and thought to cure respiratory and gastrointestinal ailments. Asian restaurants can sell a bowl of the soup for anything from $60 locally to US $1,000 overseas.

The following day, a third raid was made on a house in the Pracha Cheun area of Bangkok. Nearly 100 rare birds, as well as a collection of civets and pythons were seized along with a frozen baby orangutan found in a cooling container. Investigators believe that the orangutan was illegally shipped from Sumatra or Borneo since these are the only places where it still occurs in the wild, although in rapidly declining numbers.

The most shocking thing of all was that this level of smuggling could take place in Thailand, a country which is a signatory of the Convention on International Trade in Endangered Species of Wild Flora and Fauna (CITES), an agreement signed by more than 160 nations around the world. The alarming possibility also arose that these raids had just exposed the tip of the iceberg.

It was not the first time that Thailand had attempted to clamp down on the illegal trafficking of wild animals. Five years earlier, sporadic raids had taken place in another bid to clean up the trade after the country was once again subject to a wave of international criticism. But that campaign died down almost as quickly as it had begun. This time, with Thailand poised to host a global forum on the wildlife trade, the jury is still out on whether the raids mark a watershed in the government's attempts to stop the trade or merely another public relations exercise.

"If (police major general) Sawaek can hit the networks of big-time wildlife traffickers hard enough, then maybe he can knock them down so that they don't recover," says Dr.. Robert Mather, head of the World Wide Fund for Nature (WWF) Thailand, which is spearheading a nationwide wildlife trade campaign.

If he fails, it will go down as just another blip of enthusiasm on the long road to extinction. And since Thailand's traders buy most of their wild animals from poverty-stricken neighboring countries, the failure could have disastrous repercussions for endangered species throughout the region. 🐎

◁ *An underground trade in live Orangutans exists between Thailand and Indonesia, where many are sold illegally to supply theme parks in the region.*

# ANIMAL UNDERWORLD

Here is an analogy that illustrates why the illegal wildlife trade is so hard to stop. Picture an army of ants passing a bread crumb along a chain to an anthill. If you placed an obstacle along one route, the ants would almost certainly find an alternative way around. And if you removed one ant from the chain, another would inevitably take its place. Either way, the bread crumb will almost always reach its final destination.

So it is with the underground wildlife channels. From the major wildlife-supplying nations of Asia, home to some of the last great rainforests on earth, animals and parts almost inevitably flow to the wealthy consuming nations. In between are the transit countries, where middlemen take a cut of the profit and arrange for the illegal consignments to be delivered further down the chain.

Of all the countries in Asia, China is the biggest destination for illegal wildlife. It is the world's largest consumer of ivory, importing as much as fifteen tons each year, the equivalent of fifteen hundred dead elephants. China swallows up more than half of the ten thousand tons of freshwater turtles traded annually in the region. It is the biggest market for tiger bone, leopard cat, rhino horn, and sea horse. As an old Chinese proverb says, the nation consumes everything with "its back to the sky."

The magnitude of the problem is staggering. In 2001, China claimed a population of 1.3 billion. That is roughly five times the population of the United States. Nearly one out of every four humans lives in China. Growing prosperity has brought undreamed of buying power to the masses. If just 0.2 percent of the Chinese population earned enough money to buy a single bear gall bladder, it would take all the bears in North America to supply them.

"China is like a vacuum cleaner," says James Compton at TRAFFIC, an organization that monitors the illegal trade in the region. "It is the single greatest threat to wildlife in the whole of Asia."

While it is easy to point the finger at China, there are plenty of other culprits. The U.S. is the biggest buyer of exotic pets in the world. Nearly seven million households own a pet bird and a further four million own a pet snake, turtle, or iguana. Japan is a major purchaser of ivory. Taiwan and Korea have also used their immense wealth to acquire wild animals or products from around the region.

The supply routes begin far from these developed nations in some of the poorest and most remote parts of the region. Here the forests are still relatively intact and rare animals are easily obtainable. With just a few village contacts, a friend in the customs department, and the liberal dispensation of cash, almost anything is possible.

**Birganj, Border town
Nepal/Indian Border
January, 2004**

*The gate signifies the official border between India and Nepal and was built by Ghengis Khan. This is the major crossing point in Nepal for the smuggling of wildlife into Nepal and India.*

"China is like a vacuum cleaner," says Compton. "It is the single greatest threat to wildlife in the whole of Asia."

**Pabitora Wildlife
Sanctuary
May, 2003**

*A husband and wife of a three
member poaching team are
being transported from a
holding pen inside Patitora
Wildlife Sanctuary to the
headquarters for questioning.
Market demand and the
extremely high prices paid for
rhino horn are often difficult to
ignore for people struggling to
feed and educate themselves
in developing countries.*

Indonesia lies at the start of the trail. Rich in wildlife but impoverished in every other way, it comprises more than 17,000 islands, each of which can be used to ship out animals for profit. From this heavily populated archipelago, tens of thousands of pangolins, parrots, and other native species are illegally traded every year. Orangutans, once numbering hundreds of thousands, are now sufficiently rare that this species is likely to be the first great ape to become extinct in modern times. So many Sumatran tigers have been poached that less than 500 remain in the wild, a population that many believe is unsustainable.

"Indonesia's problems are immense," says Compton. "But at least there is recognition from the government that something needs to be done. This is always the first step towards stopping the trade."

India is another of the major suppliers, sending elephants, tigers and rhino horn to Nepal, Burma, China, and Tibet. During the 1970s, under the watchful eye of its Prime Minister Indira Gandhi, India clamped down heavily on the trade, which allowed populations of tigers and rhinos to rebound. That period ended when Gandhi was assassinated. With its long and porous borders and poor enforcement, India today provides easy pickings for wildlife traffickers

Thailand was once a major supplier. Having killed many of its own wild animals, it has now found an equally lucrative role as a transit center, where middlemen buy and sell wildlife from neighboring countries and take a hefty cut of the profits along the way.

attracted by some of Asia's last great strongholds of rare mammals.

But suppliers of wild animals need middlemen to facilitate trade and transport. That's where more developed countries like Malaysia, Thailand, and Singapore fill the void. Thailand was once a major supplier. Having killed many of its own wild animals, it has now found an equally lucrative role as a transit center, where middlemen buy and sell wildlife from neighboring countries. In Malaysia and Singapore, the trade also flourishes. Under a veneer of cooperation, the nations' shipping ports, airports, and borders are sieves allowing vast amounts of wildlife to be channelled in and out of the countries.

"Smugglers identify the loose links of the chain," says a former enforcement officer for the US government. "Their objective is to move illegal shipments with the minimum cost and the lowest risk. It's like gems or drugs or oil. It's about controlling the supply routes."

Formerly staunch communist countries like Laos and Vietnam have become the newest links in the supply chain, funneling wildlife over their porous borders into China. To avoid the more heavily enforced land routes, smugglers use private planes to fly consignments of turtles and pangolins from Kuala Lumpur, the Malaysian capital, to Vientiane in Laos. From this unregulated wildlife hub, they are sent by truck to the Vietnamese border. Shipments are also transported by boat from Indonesia to Vietnam, often transiting through intermediate destinations to avoid unwarranted attention. When officials at one border crossing clamp down on the underground channels, another one opens up to take the slack.

In the face of this global onslaught, the response from the authorities has been wholly inadequate. The loopholes available to traffickers and the weak penalties meted out to those caught only serve to facilitate the trafficking of animals. In order to contain the trade, governments have to

Monkeys are also an animal that is imported and exported in large numbers throughout China. Thirty monkeys were confiscated by the government while en route to Beijing. Ten of them had tuberculosis and over half of them had dysentery. Each one cost one hundred dollars.

◁ The illegal animal trade often goes hand in hand with transnational crime, including narcotics, trade in armaments and even trafficking in persons.

The journey from one continent to another is often a terrible ordeal for the live cargo.

Toucans with their beaks taped shut, parrots stuffed into stockings, birds that are drugged or whose eyes are perforated so that they will not sing in reaction to the light are just some of the passengers in these cruel flights.

**Guangxi Province China**

*At the Xiongsheng Bear and Tiger Mountain Village, a Chinese visitor hits a drugged Bengal tiger on the head while a laughing crowd looks.*

In remote parts of Indonesia, it is believed that the meat of a red jungle fowl will help a man to attract women and that a pangolin tongue carried in ones pocket can protect against black magic.

hit the big players who control the major routes and who are often protected by politicians. So far the powers-that-be have not done so.

In a small, crowded shop in the Tsukiji district near Tokyo's famous Fish Market, the scale and international reach of the trade is hard to ignore. Surrounded by mounted deer heads, giant turtle shells, and piles of ginseng, a stuffed polar bear wrapped in polyethylene is on sale with a price tag of US $11,000. The polar bear supposedly came from Alaska, although in the wildlife trade it is hard to corroborate such claims. Stuffed tigers, black pumas, and leopards are also up for grabs. For US $408,000, the shop will even sell a stuffed giant panda over the Internet. Asked about the blatant display and sale of endangered species, Mr. Itoi, the vendor, says that he has no problems with the police. "Buying one or two items will not hurt at all," he says. "There is no way you will be in trouble."

The same however is not true of the giant panda. Recently, seven people in China were executed for attempting to export the national animal. "I cannot display it here," says Itoi, a man in his sixties. "You can get killed for that." ✎

On the black market an adult ▷ tiger with all his component parts commands a retail price of up to US $60,000. By selling parts in richer countries, such as South Korea, Taiwan and Hong Kong, traffickers stand to make a tidy profit.

# PAPER TIGER

**Every two years, a gathering of more than a thousand conservationists and government officials takes place in one of the world's major cities. Known as the "Conference of the Parties to CITES," this is the single-most important event on the international conservation circuit. Inside vast meeting rooms, delegates from 164 countries decide which animal and plant species are threatened by the trade and which should be subject either to strict quotas or a complete ban on international trade. The resolutions agreed upon by the parties are binding with implementation to be carried out under national laws.**

CITES, or the Convention on International Trade in Endangered Species of Wild Fauna and Flora, entered into force on 1 July 1975 as the embodiment of the international community's resolve to manage uncontrolled and unsustainable international trade in plants and wildlife. To date, it has banned the commercial trade in tigers, rhinos, and 220 other species of mammals. It has also provided varying degrees of protection to more than 30,000 species of animals and plants. There is just one problem. Like any convention or set of rules, CITES is only as good as its implementation. And its resolutions have been flouted, circumvented, or ignored with impunity.

"CITES started off as a wonderful idea—something almost idealistic," says Bill Jordan, a former member of a CITES subcommittee and now head of the Bill Jordan Wildlife Defence Fund. "Its weakness is that it never had much direction; it is intergovernmental, and governments have their own agenda."

If the measure of CITES' success is its ability to halt the exploitation of species like the rhino and the elephant, then its record is less than impressive. In the early 1970s, the total rhino population was estimated at 70,000. Today it has dropped below 15,000 due to continued demand for the animal's valuable horn. The decline of elephants has been even more precipitous. In little more than a decade, close to a million elephants were massacred, largely to feed the international black market for ivory.

The problems, however, go far beyond the narrow confines of CITES. Part of the reason for the declining population of many animal species is habitat loss, an issue that the convention does not attempt to address. CITES members can also justifiably claim that not one single species covered by the convention has become extinct since it took force. Yet even when courageous

Every country in Southeast Asia is a signatory to the Convention on International Trade in Endangered Species (CITES) - except Laos.
▽

www.cites.org

decisions have been made, the sheer complexity of the rules and the existence of giant loopholes has allowed governments to exploit the situation for their own ends. For all the resolutions and endless committee meetings, CITES and the parties who enforce it have proved no match for the huge profits and minimal risks that lure smugglers into the trade.

The CITES Secretariat operates out of a United Nations building, a short drive from Geneva Airport in Switzerland. Staffed with just fifteen professional and fifteen secretarial staff, the yawning gap between the lofty expectations of the international community and the everyday reality are striking. For all its spectacular success in attracting international members, the CITES Secretariat operates on a shoestring, hamstrung in its efforts to monitor implementation of the convention and unable to pursue important policy initiatives for lack of funds. Most telling of all, the Secretariat has just one enforcement official to overlook the vital area of compliance.

How has this mighty tool of conservationists come to this? And if CITES cannot adequately fulfill the principles upon which it was founded, is it worth having at all? In addressing delegates at the twelfth Conference of the Parties in November 2002, Willem Wijnstekers, the head of the CITES Secretariat, gave a stark warning that in the absence of the necessary core funding the members seriously risked "letting down not only the many animal and plant species we appear to attach such great importance to, but the developing world in its struggle to conserve wildlife from the many threats it faces."

Growing awareness of the daunting challenges facing CITES, however, is creating the impetus for change. Spearheaded by a new generation of activists and increasingly vocal nongovernmental organizations, the parties are being forced to confront a host of controversial issues ranging from poor domestic legislation to the often questionable trading of protected animals for "research purposes." Attempts to reclaim the moral high ground and counter the influence of powerful trade lobbyists may also signal a new direction.

But even bolder action is required if they are to succeed. To solve the problems once and for all demands better regional cooperation and more effective sharing of intelligence information. It demands direct international funding assistance to poorly trained and badly paid enforcement officials; above all, it requires decisions that are based on local conservation needs rather than on the political whims of member countries.

The upcoming thirteenth Conference of the Parties to be held in Bangkok will once again put the will of CITES to the test. The member countries could successfully demonstrate that CITES does have a vital role to play as the central forum for regulating the international commercial trade in endangered species. If they fail, the killing will go on. 🐾

The problems, however, go far beyond the narrow confines of CITES. Part of the reason for the declining population of many animal species is habitat loss, an issue that the convention does not attempt to address.

# LAWLESS JUNGLES

**Thousands of miles away from the air-conditioned offices of the CITES Secretariat, in the remote Burmese town of Mongla, a young Akha trader deals openly in animal parts. Clutching a shoulder bag with pink, blue, and red tassels, he saunters from shop to shop in the cool of the late afternoon, negotiating prices with the various owners. Asked what is in his shoulder bag, he rummages among the contents then produces something that loosely resembles a piece of ginger root. However it is not ginger root but a dried tiger penis. He also has two tiger kneecaps with the texture of polished marble and the weight of pumice stone.**

The man has walked down from a village in the remote hills, a two-day journey from Mongla. He purchased the tiger parts from another hunter before coming here to sell them to one of the many shops dealing in wildlife. "The knee caps cure arthritis. The penis make you strong," he says. The price for these rare items—a mere US $80.

Situated in the northern hinterlands of Burma, a country also known as Myanmar, Mongla is a town built from heroin money. Made up of gaudy casinos, brothels, and five-star hotels, it is a beacon of wealth and prosperity surrounded by a sea of poverty and oppression. Gambling halls, concrete amphitheaters and a nine-hole golf course rise up from this valley in northern Shan state. In the ultimate irony, the town even sports an anti-drug museum.

If you have the right connections, you can leave Bangkok, the bustling capital of Thailand, in the morning and be in Mongla by the late afternoon. After an overnight in a swank hotel, you can buy a couple of tiger skins, three snow leopard skins, and a handful of tiger teeth and be back in Bangkok's Oriental Hotel for a drink on the terrace in the early evening. The following day you can fly to Hong Kong and probably make yourself a neat US $15,000 in profit, if you know the right dealers and don't get stopped by customs.

In Mongla's wildlife market, surrounded by open-air restaurants and cheap plastic tables, a dozen or so rusting wire cages are stacked on trailers. The cages contain a variety of exotic animals, their eyes peering out in horror as groups of would-be diners poke them with wooden sticks to see how much meat they have. On one trailer is a rare hornbill, one of the most beautiful creatures on earth, its gigantic yellow beak poking out of a wicker basket; on another trailer is a tawny eagle, its

In Cambodia's Tonle Sap Lake, over a ton of water snakes are harvested every day, representing the single largest snake harvest in the world. Most of the snakes are used as a cheap source of food for crocodile farms around the lake. Ironically, Siamese crocodiles, once abundant in Tonle Sap, are now virtually extinct.

—*Hunting and Wildlife Trade in Tropical and sub-tropical Asia*, Wildlife Conservation Society, 2002

**Mong La
Wa State
Burma
February, 2003**

*A man tries to sell a snake. The snakes are sold to be eaten for medicinal purposes.*

wings folded uselessly by its side. In the most pitiful condition of all is a macaque that insanely rattles the bars of its cage, driven by the pain of having its left leg torn off by a trap's steel jaws.

For the bored-looking wildlife vendor from Yunnan province in neighboring China, the catch is hardly anything out of the ordinary. "We sell whatever the hunters find in the forests," he says, pointing at the cowering animals living out their last hours cooped up in wire cages. "Come back later, and if you are lucky we may have a bear or a tiger."

Today, however the vendor is out of luck and the hunters have nothing more to offer. By nightfall, the wildlife is all gone, the macaque taken to a nearby restaurant where its skull will be sliced open while it is still alive and its brain eaten by men with chopsticks who believe that the meal will improve their intelligence. Gone too is the hornbill. Only a small eagle remains, although it too is later purchased by a group of Chinese tourists who plan to eat its eyes because they believe this will improve their eyesight.

Described in guidebooks as a land of golden temple spires and ancient cities, Burma has been virtually closed off from the outside world by one of the most repressive regimes on earth.

*The skins of tigers and leopards openly displayed in this frontier town on the Chinese border. These rare animals were supplied by local hunters and will be sold for thousands of dollars to wealthy Chinese tourists who come to Mong La to gamble and consume exotic wildlife.*

The cages contain a variety of exotic animals, their eyes peering out in horror as groups of would-be diners poke them with wooden sticks to see how much meat they have.

Despite its accession to CITES in 1977, reports of the wildlife trade within the country have been for the most part sporadic and unconfirmed. Journalists are banned from investigating the trade. Yet away from the eyes and ears of the world, the destruction of Burma's once pristine wildlife has for the most part continued.

In late 1999, a conservationist working undercover set out to collect information about the wildlife trade in Burma and the border areas of neighboring China and Thailand. Although no reliable nationwide surveys had been carried out in years, the decline in tigers, elephants, bears, otters, and turtles was alarming. Many hunters who openly confessed to killing tigers for decades, claimed that it was now virtually impossible to locate them. Those that were found were mainly smuggled across the border into China.

In the case of Mongla, the sheer volume of killing makes a mockery of attempts to stem the trade. Ruled over by a military junta and patrolled by soldiers carrying semiautomatic weapons, Mongla was until the late 1980s, simply another narco-state. But in June 1989, the generals in the capital Rangoon cut a deal with Lin Mingxian, the kingpin of Mongla, creating Special Region 4 and

**Mong La**
**February, 2003**

*A man offers an*
*endangered hornbill for*
*sale in the food market.*

granting the region virtual autonomy. The agreement has enabled the local militias to pursue their illicit activities unhindered while allowing the Burmese government to disclaim all responsibility, a situation that has continued to this day.

Back on the main street of Mongla, it's ten o'clock in the morning and Jong Hua, a fifty-something-year-old woman from northern Shan state is hard at work, selling tiger skins, and gigantic vats of cobra wine, as well as a stuffed leopard, its face frozen in a snarl. The skins are pinned up on pegs like suits in a tailor shop. Jong Hua and her husband Lio Horn, a tiger trader of more than ten years, opened the shop three years ago. They supply Chinese tourists who cross over the nearby border by the thousand every day to indulge in a fantasy world of gambling, prostitution, and wildlife.

**Mong La
February, 2003**

*In the streets of Mong La, locals attempt to sell various animal parts, including tiger penis.*

"You want to buy tiger bone wine," asks Jong Hua, suspicious at the sight of Westerners in this town that was until recently virtually off limits to foreigners. It's a foul-tasting, rust-colored concoction of tiger bone mixed with rice wine and fermented in a giant glass tank. One bottle costs US $50. The wine, says Jong Hua, is good for the health and relieves back pain. "You should drink a small quantity every day."

Visibly relaxing, the owners bring out tiger skins in such pristine condition that they could have been hauled in from the forests of Burma or neighboring India only yesterday. In one corner of the shop, there's a skin from a snow leopard that was probably trapped or electrocuted since there are no marks of death. Outside in the back of the shop, rare skins spill out of a cardboard box, their mottled colors lit up by the early morning light.

Once the skins are brought into the shop by local hunters, they are cured and treated. They are then sold either as trophies to be displayed on walls or as luxury carpets for the rich and shameless. The skins carry a price tag of US $1,000—cheap considering that there are only around 5,000 tigers left in the world. A tiger skin smuggled to the U.S. could be worth almost ten times that amount.

Here in Mongla, however, the realities of the wildlife trade are as straightforward as the kilometer-long stretch of road that leads under a giant archway to the Chinese border. There the skins and wildlife parts enter a market of 1.2 billion people who, having consumed much of their own wildlife, are draining neighboring countries to satisfy their craving for rare animals. Like a giant shop front piled high with luxury goods, Mongla openly and flagrantly dispenses illegal wildlife. And there is nothing whatsoever to stop it.

But Mongla is not a place to dally. Local Burmese are routinely interrogated. Journalists are

"Not even 1,000 yards from the border with China, vendors openly display illegal animal parts for buyers to inspect. Leopard skins and deer antlers for trophies. Dried tiger penises and bear gall bladders for traditional medicines. It's all here—for a price."

**Mong La
February, 2003**

BELOW, FAR LEFT
*Selling wildlife products in the
central market of Mong La.*

LEFT
*A python rests in the midday sun.
It will be used to take neck-draping
tourist photos for business travelers.*

simply expelled. On the way out of town, the young Akha trader with the tasselled shoulder bag is seen accompanied by a hunter carrying a wild boar's head, freshly hacked off the animal's body. As the car drives up the hill, the man is still visible in the distance, a shadowy figure holding a bloodied head in his arms, a stark reminder of the wildlife trade that continues to flourish far from the eyes of CITES members and the Western world. 🦤

THE CULTURE OF <u>KILLING</u>

# THE CULTURE OF KILLING

Thousands of years ago, a fair maiden cast herself into the raging torrents of the Mekong River to escape an arranged marriage with a magical python. She was swallowed up by the fast-flowing river, but soon returned as a mermaid-like dolphin with human-sized eyes, a beguiling smile, and a sonorous, almost musical voice. So convinced are fishermen in Laos about the truth of this ancient legend, that they go to major lengths to avoid catching a dolphin in their nets.

If dolphins are off the menu in Asia, however, just about everything else is on it, ranging from the geckos used as a treatment for persistent coughing to the boiled toad used for a toothache.

The Chinese use a word that describes this culture. *Jinbu* literally translates as "you are what you eat," and it extends to almost every wild animal. Tiger meat, bones, and genitalia are traditionally believed to provide stealth, cunning, and sexual prowess. Turtle meat is widely believed to aid longevity. Even bat hearts freshly cut out of these palpitating creatures are said by some rural communities to improve agility—and to improve asthma as a bonus.

The first references to the beneficial properties of wildlife date back almost 3,000 years. From ancient China, word of these medicinal practices spread throughout Asia. In Japan and South Korea, the term for traditional medicine literally translates as "Chinese medicine." In sixteenth-century Vietnam, the famous physician Ly Thoi Tran published a voluminous work that listed over 1,890 traditional medicine remedies of which more than 440 were obtained from wild animals, insects, and species of fish.

Some animal parts are especially noted for their remedial qualities. Deer musk, which tastes hot but has a mild medicinal effect, is regarded by traditional Chinese medicine practitioners as an essential ingredient to cure pernicious diseases of the loins, liver, and heart. The embryos of deer fawns, dried and ground into powder or steeped in alcohol, have also been widely used to cure women's urinary infections. Even tiger bone, which contains amino acids, has been found to have measurable anti-inflammatory effects.

But while many animal parts and herbs used in traditional Chinese medicine have scientifically proven properties, much of the wildlife trade is based solely on local superstition. In Cambodia, the Khmer people buy elephant tails in the hope that they will help to stop nightmares. In parts of Laos, a concoction of leaf monkey, porcupine's stomach, and bamboo consumed with alcohol is said to

Tradition has it that the adrenaline generated by pain and fear enhances the quality of the meat.

**Guangzou China**

*Dogs being processed for sale in the Guangzhou animal market. The conditions and treatment of animals in this market, the biggest in Asia, are horrific.*

infuse the local people with the power of the trees. Meanwhile in China, hundreds of tons of shark fins, snakes, and turtles are eaten every year in the belief that they contain unique medicinal qualities.

The sale of many rare animals is now illegal throughout Asia. But it is likely to take time for people to discard beliefs and superstitions that have been embraced for countless generations. Despite the occasional clampdown by the authorities, it is still easier to find wild animals in the markets of Indonesia or Southern China than it is in the forests. "Many Chinese believe that by eating wildlife parts they will increase their strength and sexual power," says Hardi Baktiantoro, a conservationist from ProFauna Indonesia. "There is little evidence that this is true."

If only it was just ignorance fueling this bizarre obsession with wildlife, it could eventually be solved with education—much in the way it was in Europe. In the case of Asia, however, vast increases in human population combined with growing affluence are driving ever-larger numbers of animals down the road to extinction. In many countries the consumption of wildlife is seen as the ultimate display of wealth and status. Influential businessmen and government bureaucrats have been known to flaunt their connections by ordering anything from live bears lowered on to red-hot coals to raccoons boiled alive in vats of hot water. Tradition has it that the adrenaline generated by pain and fear enhances the quality of the meat. And the rarer and more expensive the animal, the bigger the demand.

If only it was just ignorance fueling this bizarre obsession with wildlife, it could eventually be solved with education—much in the way it was in Europe. In the case of Asia, however, vast increases in human population combined with growing affluence are driving ever-larger numbers of animals down the road to extinction.

In Indonesia, which is host to more than 500 species of mammals and 1,500 species of birds, wildlife is never far from the menu. As twilight descends on Lokasari, a sprawling Chinese district in northern Jakarta, Ismail, a woman in her fifties is hawking snake, goat's testicles, monitor lizard, and the diminutive ant-eating creatures known as pangolins. In a country where superstitions are widespread and medical treatment prohibitively expensive, Ismail claims to have no shortage of customers for her culinary curiosities. "There is nothing bad about selling wild animals because they are good for the health and because there are plenty where they come from," she says.

But Ismail is wrong. The medicinal value of a pangolin scale is no greater than that of the hair-like particles from which it is made. The level of protein in the pangolin's meat is similar to that of pork. Ismail is also badly misinformed on another count. Pangolins have been so widely hunted over the past decade that this friendly nocturnal creature has seen its population virtually wiped out in many parts of Southeast Asia. ➜

**Bangkok, Thailand
February, 2003**

*At one of the many shark fin soup restaurants in Chinatown, customers select shark fin to be prepared for soup.*

LEFT
*A chef prepares shark fin soup for customers.*

RIGHT
**Medan, Indonesia
October, 2003**
*A bat hunter displays his recently caught flying foxes by the roadside. The bats are from the forest surrounding Medan and are a local delicacy.*

# TIGERS FOR SALE

At the Sri Racha Tiger Zoo in Thailand's gulf region, the "amazing tiger show" is already in full swing. As an orangutan dressed in shorts, red T-shirt and suspenders pulls a Bengal tiger along on a go-cart, the assembled crowd bursts into spontaneous applause. Other tricks follow in quick succession. Tigers stand on their hind legs begging like dogs, walk tightropes, and, in a grand finale, leap through flaming hoops. Outside the fenced off circus ring, an "African" dressed in leopard skins poses with two of the tigers who dawdle submissively in a corner, shielded behind thick panes of glass. The fact that tigers are not native to the African continent attracts barely a whisper.

Named after the nearby seaside village, the Sri Racha Zoo is more than just an open theme park and a second-rate circus. Acclaimed as a world-famous breeding center, its 120 acres play host to more than 100,000 crocodiles—as well as ostriches, single-hump camels, elephants, pigs, and scorpions. Set up by a well-connected Thai businessman, the zoo has a license that allows it to keep large numbers of tigers. However, the zoo is forbidden from trading or selling animals for commercial purposes.

That has not stopped the owner from exporting these protected animals. On Christmas Eve 2002, while families around the world sang carols and wrapped presents, a consignment of 100 tigers was flown from Thailand to the tropical island of Hainan in Southern China. The animals, with a declared value of US $2500 apiece, were part of a bigger shipment of 2,000 Siamese crocodiles destined for the Sanya Love World theme park.

On December 26, two days after their arrival, a Chinese news agency quoted a theme park executive as saying that the tigers would initially be used for breeding purposes, but that if laws were to change they could be offered as food for tourists with a taste for the exotic. Although a company spokesman subsequently retracted the statement after an international uproar, it failed to stem suspicions that a major act of illegal trade had taken place under the very eyes of the Thai and Chinese authorities.

It was not the first controversy involving the Sri Racha Tiger Zoo. In December 2000, investigators from the London-based Environmental Investigation Agency (EIA) discovered that tiger bone pills were illegally being sold on the premises in the Sri Racha Traditional Health Clinic. Several months earlier, the Chinese owner of a pharmaceutical store in Bangkok told undercover

**Sri Racha Tiger Zoo
Chon Buri, Thailand
February, 2003**

*Inside the tiger nursery,
tourists can have their
photograph taken
with a tiger cub for
150 baht (US $3.60).*

investigators that he bought tiger parts from the Sri Racha Tiger Zoo.

When asked to explain how the tigers had been sent to China in apparent violation of the Thai Wildlife Preservation and Protection Act, Forestry Department officials scratched their heads. Others blamed interference from higher levels. The signature at the bottom of the documents confirmed that the head of Thailand's CITES team himself had given the go-ahead in accordance with provisions allowing trade for research and exhibition purposes.

Even more surprising, while every year the Si Racha Tiger Zoo claims to breed up to 100 tiger cubs, the zoo still only has around 400 tigers in total. It's not clear where all the other tigers have gone.

The farming of tigers is far from unique. During the 1980s and early 1990s special tiger-breeding farms sprang up in Thailand and China. These intended to supply factories that mass-produced tiger-bone medicines for the local and international market. The farms turned into tourist attractions after national trade bans put an end to the breeders' hopes. In Guangxi Province in China, visitors could pay to hit a drugged Bengal tiger in the head in front of crowds of laughing spectators. Yet despite all the fun and games as well as blanket denials by all parties, tigers continued to be bred

◁ "We estimate the number of tigers at no more than 5,000 or 6,000," says Dr. Tony Lynam, at the Wildlife Conservation Society's office in Bangkok, which has carried out extensive camera-trapping surveys of tiger populations in much of Asia. If correct, it means more than 95 percent of the world's tiger population has been wiped out over the past 100 years.

Even though tigers in the wild spend about 12 to 14 hours of their day sleeping, the remainder of their time is spent hunting and patrolling their territory. When they are in captivity, these activities are out of the question. The result is that many tigers in captivity "pace" their cages.

**Chon Buri**
**February, 2003**

*At the Sri Racha Tiger Zoo in Chonburi, tiger cubs are suckled on pigs so that the mother tiger can continue to breed uninterrupted.*

Tiger bones are used in many Chinese medicines. Plaster made from tiger bone and musk (from the endangered musk deer), combined with menthol, is said to be effective against rheumatism. Chinese medical books also claim that tiger bone is effective against ulcers, typhoid, malaria, dysentery and burns. Some of the more outlandish prescriptions are for prolapse of the anus, fright, evil influences and guarding new-born children from infection.

in captivity in Asia with their bones illegally sold to medicine shops throughout the region.

Driving the trade are huge potential profits. Every part of the tiger has value, from the tail that is ground up and mixed with soap for use in skin disease ointment to the whiskers that are used as protective charms. Tiger bones can sell for US $400 per kilogram and claws for US $150 apiece. In the late 1990s, a Japanese manufacturer even produced a brand of tiger penis pills, which went on sale for US $27,000 per bottle. In one of the great ironies of the wildlife trade, tigers are worth considerably more dead than alive.

The big hope now for tiger farm operators is that the international commercial trading ban on these animals will eventually be lifted. Such a development, they claim, could save tigers in the wild. But the argument is as cynical as it is short-sighted. The average cost of raising one tiger to maturity is estimated at US $2,000. A bullet costs less than US $1. Users of traditional Chinese medicine also believe that wild animals provide more effective tonics than farmed animals. Since it is difficult and costly to distinguish between the bones of a wild tiger and a captive-bred tiger, any change in the law would almost inevitably lead to an upsurge in poaching. "Tiger farming simply increases demand," says Debbie Banks, a wildlife campaigner at the EIA. "In turn, this encourages more killing."

**Luang Prabang**
**Laos**

*Large tiger shot by villagers.*

# ANCIENT HISTORY

High up on the precipitous sandstone cliffs of Pha Taem in northeast Thailand, a succession of prehistoric paintings extends around the hillside. The ochre paintings, which date back some 2,000 to 4,000 years, depict human figures as well as giant catfish, elephants, turtles, and primitive-looking animal traps. Drawn with animal blood and mixed with vegetable gum and local soil, they are believed by archaeologists to be among the oldest cave paintings in the region as well as some of the first to show hunter-gatherers at work.

For thousands of years, man has hunted and traded wild animals for food, for profit, and for pleasure. In 400 B.C., a Greek physician is said to have transported a plum-headed parrot from India to teach it Greek. The physician's keen interest in wildlife was shared by other Europeans. Alexander the Great reportedly sent an Indian elephant to his old tutor Aristotle, whose fascination with the anatomy of animals can be gauged by his composition of nearly fifty volumes on zoology. By 21 B.C., large numbers of tigers, tortoises, and even a python had been shipped to the island of Samos, where they were received by the Emperor Augustus.

The great birds and mammals of Asia were prized as more than just scientific specimens to be wheeled out in public on special occasions. So enamored with white elephants was King Narai of Siam that he honored them with splendid sonorous names and lavished every form of luxury upon them, from special attendants who burned incense to sweeten the air to musicians who played soothing music to help them sleep. When Fernao Mendes Pinto, a Portuguese adventurer visited Ayutthaya in 1545, he observed a white elephant being taken down to bathe in the river, shaded from the sun by twenty-four servants carrying white parasols and guarded by 3,000 armed men.

If early hunting methods were primitive, relying on traps, clubs, and spears tipped with bone, later generations soon perfected their skills. Akbar the Great, the legendary Mogul emperor kept 1,000 trained cheetahs with which to hunt antelope. On one notable occasion, he surrounded an area of sixty square miles with 10,000 soldiers and spent the next two months hunting game with only a sword, a bow and arrow and a spear. His successor Jehangir was even more prolific and distinguished himself by killing a total of 889 wild buffalo in addition to many other types of wildlife.

By the thirteenth century, the trade in wildlife in Asia was already well established. When the Chinese emissary Chou Ta-Kuan visited Cambodia in 1297, he observed a thriving market in tigers,

"Normally on tour, His High Highness attends to correspondence and office work from 10am to 4pm. After lunch, if there is a ringed tiger, he sallies forth to enjoy it."

—E A Smythies in a sporting diary for the Maharaja Joodha Shumshere of Nepal, 1942

**The Maharaja
Nepal
Early 1900's**

*Shumshere, King of Nepal,
poses on the massive head of an
Indian one horned rhinoceros.*

*The Maharaja Shumshere, King
of Nepal, displays the total kill
for one hunting season.*

"Hunting is a glorious
sort of vice working
its narcotic with all
the efficacy of the
ubiquitous poppy."

—*Colonel Charles
Askins, Asian Jungle-
African Bush. 1959*

panthers, bears, wild boars, stags, and gibbons. "The most sought-after products are the feathers of the kingfisher, elephant tusks, rhinoceros horns, and beeswax," he wrote in his celebrated account *Customs of Cambodia*, which was first published in 1312. According to Chou, who spent a year in the country, light-colored and veined rhinoceros horns were especially highly regarded together with tusks from an elephant freshly killed by spears.

Part of the reason for the popularity of rhino horn was its use in the making of ceremonial goblets. The Chinese believed that if poison was placed in a goblet made from the horn of a male rhino, the liquid would magically froth. Such was the level of treachery in the early kingdoms of China that these beautifully carved goblets became an indispensable item for use in oath-taking ceremonies. By the beginning of the fourteenth century, China boasted an imperial workshop in which 150 craftsmen did nothing else but make objects from rhino horn and ivory.

There was, however, another reason for this animal's widespread popularity. The male rhino's sexual proclivities were legendary. Mating could last for anything from twenty minutes to several hours and be repeated several times a day. The secret to these exertions was believed to lie in the rhino horn, which weighed up to a kilogram and was made from densely matted rough hair. As a result, powdered rhino horn became known in some circles as the ultimate aphrodisiac, a belief that has since been widely disproved.

Other healing properties were also ascribed to the rhino. Chinese pharmacists commonly recommended the use of rhino horn and hooves as a remedy for leprosy, snakebites, and venereal diseases. Rhino urine was consumed as a cure for asthma and the oil from rhino skin for bellyache and deafness. "It is generally known that the hunting of rhino is very much stimulated by the great value attributed to almost all parts of the rhino's body," noted a Dutch author at the beginning of the twentieth century. One of the most miraculous claims came from India. Pregnant women were advised that they could alleviate birth pangs by placing a rhino horn under the bed. As a result, rhino horns would commonly be rented out to expectant mothers.

Meanwhile, the fame of the strange looking rhinoceros had already spread further afield. In the early sixteenth century, the emperor of Cambay, one of the many states in India, presented the Portuguese King Emmanuel with a great one-horned rhino as a gift. Wanting to test this strange animal's strength, the king put it in a ring with an elephant. The elephant fled the moment that it spotted the one-horned creature. The king was delighted by the novelty of the rhino and decided to present it to Pope Leo X. The ship carrying the rhino, however, was hit by a storm and capsized.

# KILLING EPIDEMIC

The Oxford English dictionary has a definition for the verb "plunder." It means to obtain booty by force, to seize valuable goods, to steal, or to loot. Few words in the English language sum up so well the situation in Asia in the seventeenth and eighteenth centuries. It must have been extraordinary to see ships piled high with tamed elephants, tigers, buffalo, birds of paradise, and deer skins sailing across the great oceans to China, Japan, and the Indian states around the Bay of Bengal. In gigantic holding pens on the quayside at Aceh as many as twenty elephants at a time were crowded together, awaiting transport to far-off continents like lambs to the slaughter.

Such was the scale of the plunder that special ships had to be built to accommodate the animals freshly plucked from the jungles of Asia. If the conditions of slave boats are anything to go by, their plight must have been horrific. Crammed into tiny spaces and chained at the feet, the stench of urine and feces would have filled the vessel with unutterable squalor. Many of the animals died on these long desolate voyages, riddled by diseases. Some escaped their manacles and fell overboard. Of the animals that left port, barely 60 percent survived the journey. But the enormous profits more than made up for these short-term mishaps.

The industrial age of colonization upped the ante as never before. In the name of progress, Asian countries were stripped of their economic wealth on a scale that defies imagination. Once mighty tracts of rainforest were torn down to build railways and bridges. In their place, the great torchbearers of civilization left behind a bleached and denuded landscape.

Between 1875 and 1925, at least 80,000 tigers were killed in India alone—a feat so catastrophic that it recalled the great buffalo killings of North America in which an entire species was virtually wiped out in little more than three decades. In this case, however, the slaughter took place after the British colonial masters declared the tiger a pest and offered bounties for its head. Other types of wildlife, including at least 150,000 leopards, were also indiscriminately shot as Indian princes, British officers, and civil servants rampaged through the forests. It was as if wildlife had been reduced to a commodity, mercilessly hunted for money or for pleasure.

**Nepal**
**Early 1900s**

*Royal hunting party rallies on elephant back.*

The scale of the killing was all the more terrifying given the special reverence that Indians held for any life-form—a concept known as *ahimsa*, meaning the avoidance of harm. Elephants were venerated as symbols of Ganesh, the Hindu god of wisdom. Tigers were worshipped as guardians of the jungle, credited with mystical powers and believed to sprout wings in order to travel vast distances.

Religious beliefs and superstitions, however, did little to save the animals of the Indian subcontinent. In a small studio in Kathmandu owned by Kiran Manchitrakar, the grandson of one of Nepal's most famous court photographers, there is a black-and-white photograph of that era. It shows an austere-looking man lined up against a backdrop of around 180 tiger, leopard, and crocodile skins. The photograph is faded, the picture of a bygone era. But the formal attire, the stiff collars and top hats, give the appearance more of a pheasant shoot on an English summer's day than of a gigantic culling of some of the world's rarest species of wildlife. The man in the photo is the Maharaja Shumshere, the King of Nepal and the display of animals and skins, the total kill for one season.

To ensure that he wasted no time in pursuit of his prey, the Maharaja would commonly send out seven or eight groups of *shikaris*, or seasoned beaters, to scour the forest-clad foothills in search of tiger tracks. Once a tiger or a rhino had been spotted, members of the shooting party mounted on up to 200 elephants would encircle the animal. As the cornered beast charged the solid wall of elephants, the Maharaja and his favored guests would spring forward and dispatch it with a blast of the rifle.

The relish with which the maharajas went about hunting in this remote corner of the Himalayas was also shared by British royals. In 1911, Queen Elizabeth's grandfather, King George V visited Nepal, where he and a large entourage spent three days hunting in the jungle. King George reportedly shot one of eighteen rhinos as well as several tigers. Ten years later, the Prince of Wales also joined the Maharaja Joodha Shumshere on one of his infamous shoots. So close is the historical relationship between the two countries that when Queen Elizabeth II visited Nepal in 1961, she was presented with a 2.5-meter tusk that was intricately carved by one of the country's most famous family artisans. 🐗

# THE GREAT WHITE HUNTER

On the outskirts of Chiang Rai in northern Thailand, there is a house that belongs to the son of a great white hunter. Surrounded by leafy gardens and orchards, it is far removed from the jungles of Laos where Jean Dauplay and his father hunted wild animals with shotguns and homemade cartridges in the early part of the twentieth century. But Jean, now 100 years old, still recalls those days, his voice trembling as he relives the memories. "We would wait in line as the animals were driven out of the forest by up to 200 villagers at a time banging drums," he says, gesturing into the distance as if the once-plentiful herds of cattle and gaur were concealed by the lush vegetation. "We would choose the most beautiful, the most proud, and the most savage of all the wild animals—and then we would shoot."

Sometimes it was wild pigs or panthers that emerged from the forest clearings, rampaging through the undergrowth as the hunters hurriedly raised their rifles to fire. On other occasions, it was the stag deer, considered the most stealthy and intelligent of all animals. But for Jean, who worked for a European trading company, it was that split second before he pulled the trigger that summed up all that was noble and good about the sport as man faced off against the wild beast. "It was one hunter against another," he says. "If you missed, the animal could kill you."

Jean has a diary that documents some of those early hunting exploits. Written by his father Jean Jacque, the French representative to Laos, it lists the weapons, the animals, and the places visited by the "great white hunter." "27 Oct. 1907: Left at five in the morning accompanied by two coolies," records the aging manuscript. "In the evening Mr. Villard kills a stag deer." "Oct. 28: Passed a group of 15 wild boar. Killed one with a shot from my 400."

**Jean Dauplay**

Jean remembers one incident in particular. He was in the remote province of Saravane in southern Laos with his father when reports came of a man-eating tiger that had attacked and mauled four Buddhist monks as they collected food and offerings in the early morning. With great courage, his father cornered the animal outside a village and killed it with a blast from his shotgun. Once the animal was dead, the hunting party removed the skin, leaving the meat and intestines for the villagers. "You must understand that there was something special about being a hunter," says Jean. "Nothing else mattered."

These days, Jean can no longer read the diary or see the accompanying photographs. His eyes are fading, his voice is barely a whisper, and for much of the time he is restricted to a wicker chair. He gave up hunting in the 1950s, when he mistakenly shot a gibbon, the most human-like of all the animals. "It cried like a person—so I stopped," he says. "I have never hunted since that time."

While Jean turned his back on hunting, the killing continued, aided by new roads, more accurate weapons, and the onset of war. Bill Young, a big, bearded American-born serviceman, also witnessed the profusion of wildlife during those times. Flying low over Laos in the early 1960s, he would marvel at the herds of wild cattle, gaur, elephants and colonies of monkeys running amok through the plains and forest clearings. Cut off from its neighbors by soaring mountain chains and virgin forests, this remote Buddhist country was for many Westerners the closest Asia got to an earthly paradise. "There was something almost biblical about it," he says. "Wildlife was so plentiful, it was as if God had put it on earth to nourish man. Nobody could ever believe that one day it would almost all be gone."

Year by year, however, the mighty animals that gave Laos the title "Lane Xiang—Land of a Million Elephants" were to disappear, victims of the ongoing war between the communists and

**Saravane, Laos
Early 1900s**

*Dauplay posing with the man-eater that devoured four monks on their rounds collecting alms. The villagers believed it was possessed. They called upon Dauplay, (a resident and the local French official) to kill it.*

"I fear that the situation will get worse before it gets better," says Sir David Attenborough. "Instead of controlling the environment for the benefit of the population, maybe we should control the population to ensure the survival of the environment."

*Dauplay posing with the man-eater.*

U.S.-backed troops. The biggest devastation took place in the remote hills, where a secret war was fought by hill tribe militias armed and financed by the Americans. But even on the lush plains around the capital Vientiane, the sounds of birds and parrots was gradually replaced by silence. For Young, a giant of a man with a passion for wildlife, the slow death of this Garden of Eden is one of the great untold tragedies of the conflict. By the mid-1970s, Laos had largely been emptied of its wildlife with large tracts of forest reduced to scrubland.

The destruction continued through much of Indochina, as bombs rained down on the former hunting grounds of colonials, reducing the great forests and animals to ashes. In April 1975, when the Cambodian capital Phnom Penh fell to the invading Khmer Rouge, an even bigger slaughter began. Overshadowed by the killing of between 1 million and 3 million Cambodians, the Khmer Rouge and their Chinese advisers emptied the country's forests of some of their most valuable resources in order to fund their fanatical war. During a two-year period at least 29 tons of deer horn, 6 tons of monkey bones, 1.5 tons of elephant bones, 7 tons of pangolin scales, and 2 tons of tortoise shells were shipped to China for use in traditional medicine. That was in addition to thousands of dried geckos, tiger skins, and bears. The bloody proceeds came to the Khmer Rouge in the form of artillery, guns, and ammunition—used to prolong the reign of one of the most brutal regimes in history.

Many rare skins from Asia also found their way to Europe and the U.S., where rampant consumption encouraged the slaughter of animals in these far-off lands. Beautifully mottled pelts of clouded leopards and tigers were made into rugs while cheetah skins were used for shoes, handbags, and wallets sold throughout Europe. Only when the tidal wave of skins began to dry up did the enormity of the killing finally strike home.

By the late 1960s and early 1970s, the complacency that had long gripped the world had been shattered. Shocked by the massacres taking place in far-off countries and the images of protesters burning tiger skin coats in the streets of London and Paris, governments introduced a flurry of conservation measures. By the early 1980s, hunting in many parts of Asia was in decline, but the damage had already been done. The last known tiger on the island of Bali was shot in 1937. The last cheetah in central India was sighted in 1952. In China, home to one of the richest and most diverse populations of wildlife on earth, the once vast tracts of forest were almost empty.

Since the 1980s, a combination of education and high-profile campaigns waged in public have raised awareness of the need for conservation to new heights. In schools around Asia, children are taught that animals form a part of their natural heritage and should have the right to exist in the same way that they do. Around national parks, local people are taught that wildlife is a vital part of their everyday lives.

However, the enormous profits involved in wildlife smuggling together with improved transportation networks and better communications have also spawned a darker side to the trade. As increased prosperity takes hold in the region, a gigantic international market for wildlife products has opened up, threatening to drive ever-larger numbers of species to the brink of extinction. 🐆

*Dauplay with a hunting party.*

**Hunting Expeditions
Saravane, Laos
Early 1900's**

LEFT
*The hunting party—surrounded by Lao Theung (indigenous people of that area) in Southeast Laos—with a "Banteng", a large wild cattle of SE Asia and now a protected species.*

TOP AND BOTTOM RIGHT
*Gathering of hunters and killed "Krating" or Gaur, a large wild cattle of SE Asia—also now a protected species.*

# The Wildlife Collector

Some people collect cuckoo clocks. Other people collect Ming dynasty porcelain or Georgian silver tankards. But there is a man who has made a career out of amassing rare horns and antlers.

Prasert Sri Yongtong is literally obsessed with these appendages. He has dozens of pairs of critically endangered Eld's deer hanging above his toilet in his four-storied concrete apartment block. He has the antlers of the now extinct Schomburgk's deer hanging above the microwave oven in his kitchen—each pair conservatively worth in excess of US $10,000. And he has horns from the kouprey and just about every other exotic hoofed animal throughout Asia scattered throughout this building and his nearby house. All told, they probably represent one of the biggest collections of antlers and horns in the world.

But that's not all. In his sitting room, the fifty-three-year-old Thai eccentric has the skull of a Sumatran rhino; on the floor, two enormous elephant heads; and in a glass cabinet, a collection of fossilized shark teeth. In fact the wealthy Thai collector has so many wildlife items and parts that he doesn't even know how many there are.

"There are something in the region of 3,000 to 4,000 pieces here," he says, waving absentmindedly at a bathroom piled high with banteng, gaur, and saola horns and antlers. "Whenever I see rare antlers in other people's houses, I ask to buy them."

The initial urge to collect came at the age of ten when the young boy began gathering horns from friends of the family and neighbors. By his late twenties, Prasert was so fascinated by these animal parts that he began traveling around the country in search of valuable specimens. Since then he has visited India, Pakistan, Burma, Laos and Cambodia—among other countries—to add to his priceless collection. "My plan is to open a museum so that other people can appreciate it," he says. "When I am eighty or ninety years old, I want this to be my legacy."

Perhaps the rarest thing about Prasert's collection is that he claims it is legal. That's because many of the horns and antlers were acquired years ago, well before wildlife laws outlawed the buying and selling of endangered species. As such they provide a rich documentary record of hoofed-animal species, many of which, like the Schomburgk's deer or kouprey, have either ceased to exist or are on the brink of extinction.

It's the same obsession to possess something rare and unique that is driving a new generation of collectors to break the law in order to get their hands on wildlife species. Some collectors are wealthy generals or rich businessmen. Others are ornithologists or zoologists who appreciate the beauty of the natural species and want to keep them for themselves.

When U.K. police raided the home of thirty-four-year-old Derek Lee in the north of England, they found seventy-eight protected bird eggs hidden under the drawers of two cabinets along with an egg-blowing kit and various notebooks containing sketches of bird's nests. A self-confessed ornithologist, it was Lee's third conviction for egg-related offenses. Lee was sentenced to three months in jail. But most illegal collectors remain at large. "What we need is tougher enforcement," says Dr. Barbara Maas, head of Care for the Wild International, a U.K.-based charity. "If governments and people are serious about stopping the illegal wildlife trade, there is an enormous amount that can be done."

Thanks to campaigns and appeals by Care for the Wild International and a number of other conservation groups, the public is gradually waking up to the threat caused by buyers of exotic animals. It's only a small step, but one that is vital to ensure the survival of many protected animals. Without more stringent penalties and tighter enforcement, some of the world's last great bird, mammal, and amphibian species could end up as specimens in people's houses.

# PICKLED VIPERS

In a narrow alleyway off Hang Vai Street in the Vietnamese capital Hanoi, Mr. Quang is drinking his first snake cocktail of the day. Seated in a small shophouse surrounded by jars of pickled vipers, gently fermenting cobras, and potent rattlesnake wine, he sips the yellowish liquid, tasting the mixture of rice wine and herbs, before knocking back the glass. For Quang, a native of Hanoi, there is nothing unusual about snake consumption. Quang's father, who has drunk snake wine and eaten snake heart and blood for much of his life, is now a healthy old man. Quang too has few doubts about the medicinal properties of these writhing creatures. "Snake make mans very strong," he says in faulting English, flexing his nether regions and smiling contentedly.

Every year, the Vietnamese and the Chinese consume an estimated 10,000 tons of snakes, purportedly to cure bone diseases and stomach problems, but also because they are considered an aphrodisiac. Most people believe that the more poisonous the snake, the more effective its healing properties. King cobras and black cobras are especially prized, despite the fact that villagers regularly die of snakebites. The most expensive and popular organ is the heart, which continues to beat for several minutes after it has been cut out of the live animal and placed in a glass mixed with alcohol.

So profitable is the snake trade in Vietnam and China that rice farmers often find it more remunerative to collect these reptiles than to work as laborers in the fields. And so big is demand from people like Mr. Quang that entire villages have turned to breeding snakes, many of which are transported over the border to China. The love affair with snakes, however, has had an unfortunate side effect. Large numbers of snake species are now at risk of disappearing forever—raising the prospects of an epidemic of rats and other rodents that could destroy their crops.

Even that is not yet worrying the locals. In the remote province of Bac Lieu in southern Vietnam, entrepreneurial villagers have hit upon a solution. Every morning thousands of farmers head out into the fields to gather rats, which they sell for human consumption. Depending on the type of rat, the meat costs anywhere from US $0.30 to US $2 per kg. The meat, renowned for its sweet flavor, is generally served fried or grilled, or boiled in soup.

With a burgeoning Asian middle class, some turtle species, after having survived since before the dinosaurs, now face near certain extinction within ten years time.

Snake bile has long been valued as a tonic, characterized ▷
by its sweet aftertaste. The bile is mixed with rice wine
and consumed before a meal as an invigorating beverage,
an appetite stimulant and an aphrodisiac. In the treatment
of diseases, snake bile is used for whooping cough,
rheumatic pain, high fever, convulsions, hemorrhoids,
gum bleeding and skin infections.

Fearing for the country's fast-dwindling population of animals, Prime Minister Phan Van Khai has now ordered the closure of restaurants selling protected wildlife, a move that threatens to deprive the country of some of its most favored types of cuisine. But such is the lucrative nature of the business that hungry Hanoians continue to feast on such delicacies as snake gall bladder, pangolin, and boiled dog with lemongrass.

At the far end of town from where Mr. Quang drinks his snake wine, another cog in the wildlife trade is thriving. Inside a shophouse showcasing a stuffed deer and a stuffed bear, Dr. Doan Cung, a gray-haired practitioner of traditional Chinese medicine, extols the virtues of some of the country's most endangered animals. For liver disease or hepatitis, Dr. Doan recommends taking a small vial of bear bile mixed with runny honey every couple of days. He suggests treating heart disease with powdered rhino horn, and claims that old people with fragile bones will benefit from the compounds found in tiger bone that is boiled until it turns into a thick *cao*, or jelly. "Animals are better for human beings than herbs," he says as he unloads a bag of frozen deer horn from the refrigerator. "Depending on the disease, there is always an animal that is suitable."

Obtaining rare wildlife, however, is considerably more difficult and expensive than it was a

**Hanoi, Vietnam
November, 2003**

*Snake whisky on sale
in Hanoi. This is a very
common product in
Vietnam and is sold
quite openly.*

few years ago, laments Dr. Doan. To ensure a steady supply of these precious parts, the veteran physician, now in his seventies, must rely on a network of local contacts. Tiger bone, he claims comes from Vietnam or neighboring countries, where the creatures are more abundant. Rhino horn can be purchased from villagers in the famous Cat Tien National Park, where a handful of the animals were rediscovered several years ago and where horns have probably been stockpiled by villagers and powerful military officials for many decades longer.

Sitting in this cramped shophouse talking to this delightful old man with his red cross cap and spectacles, it is easy to forget that these supposed cures are draining the forests of their last wild animals—or that herbal remedies can now cure many of the most virulent diseases—rendering the use of wildlife unnecessary. Here in Vietnam, however, such reasoning has largely fallen on deaf ears.

In one of the most stomach-churning practices still common in the north, bear carcasses are fermented in giant glass tanks filled with rice wine. The resulting mud-colored liquor is believed to bring good health and sexual power and is especially popular among men.

For his part Mr. Quang sees little reason to change his ways despite the growing international outcry. "If you are sick and animal cures you, then why not eat animal?" he asks with the far-off happy look of a budding philosopher. 🐢

**Hanoi
November, 2003**

RIGHT
*Vietnamese mafia
make a toast with
glasses of snake bile.*

BOTTOM RIGHT
**Snake Wine
Phunc Hiep,
Mekong Delta
Vietnam**

The Golden Box Turtle grows to around 20 centimeters in length but ▷ can fetch US $1,200 per kilogram. Believed to cure a host of ailments from cancer to kidney failure, it was for centuries regarded as a symbol of good fortune and royalty.

For centuries, humans have killed ▷ pythons out of fear. Snakes of all kinds are also hunted for food, skins, and blood. Live snakes are killed to order in Thai markets so customers can drink the fresh blood, thought to impart vitality. Python and other snake skins are made into fashionable accessories such as purses, shoes, and belts. More recently, snakes have become sought after for the pet trade and for zoos.

# BEAR FARMING

**"Blind,"** an Asiatic black bear, has spent seven years in a cage barely larger than his outstretched body. His stomach carries the scars of an operation to extract bile that went badly wrong. His eyes stare out vacantly at identical rows of cages that extend on either side.

Every three or four months, Blind is drugged with a syringe full of ketamine, which is fired into his side from a blowpipe. The barely conscious bear, his jaws twitching and his eyes still open, is hauled from his cage onto a metal cradle and wheeled into an adjoining "operating room." Using an ultrasound machine, the owner locates the bear's valuable gall bladder, the organ that temporarily stores bile secreted by the liver. Once the gall bladder is found, a 10-cm surgical needle is plunged into the animal's flesh and the green bile is pumped out into a glass beaker.

In all the operation takes little more than fifteen minutes before the bear is manhandled back into his cage. It will take another thirty minutes for him to fully come around. The 250ccs of bile that Blind produces can be sold for around US $1,000 for use in traditional Chinese medicine, where it is widely prescribed as a cure for hepatitis and hangovers as well as chronic diarrhea, hemorrhoids, and eye problems.

Blind is just one of seventy bears locked away in this illegal farm in Ha Tay Province, northern Vietnam. His fellow bears include "Circus," a fully grown moon bear sold to the owner by a

fairground in Hanoi because she performed tricks badly, and "Finance," a gleaming well-kept 200-kg bear that once belonged to a banker. "I have names for all the bears," says Mrs. Loc, the Chinese owner who started up the farm with two bears and now operates one of the biggest so-called experimental bear-breeding centers in the country.

She might just as well be referring to a bunch of pedigree dogs in kennels—except that these endangered animals almost all come from the wild. Typically the mothers are shot or trapped by wire snares in the forests of Laos and Vietnam. The whimpering and disoriented cubs are concealed in bags and smuggled to nearby towns where they are sold to traders. Bears may change hands

When South Korea hosted the 1988 Olympic games, it was widely reported that 30 sun bears were smuggled into the capital (Seoul) and their gall bladders used to boost the performance of South Korea's athletes.

LEFT
**Hanoi**
**Vietnam**
**November, 2003**

*At an illegal bear farm, the freshly extracted bear bile is placed in a jar ready for distribution.*

RIGHT
*At the same farm, after tranquilization, the bear is removed from its cage in order to have its bile drained by needle from its gall bladder.*

several times before they find a long-term home. With the exception of those butchered to supply restaurants that sell bear paws, they almost always end their days in one of the many farms like this.

Bear bile "farming" was first introduced in North Korea in the early 1980s in a bid to stop bears being taken from the wild and killed for their gall bladders. Today it is a lucrative industry involving at least 4,000 bears in Vietnam and probably two or three times as many in China. Until recently, it was common for 13- to 18- centimeter metal catheters to be surgically implanted into the bear's gall bladder to ensure a continuous supply of bile. This cruel method, however, caused excruciating pain and often led to chronic infection, with bears dying after less than ten years of captivity. Their normal life span in the wild is thirty years.

The use of ultrasound machines revolutionized the industry by allowing bears to be kept alive longer and by dispelling some of the fiercest criticism that the animals were being treated cruelly. But this supposedly humane and painless form of extraction can still lead to the harmful leakage of bile into the body and to a slow, agonizing death from peritonitis, a severe form of inflammation.

"Whatever technique is used to extract bile from live bears is absolutely horrific," says Jill Robinson, founder of the Hong Kong-based Animals Asia Foundation, an organization dedicated to putting an end to this practice. Robinson first witnessed the horrors of bear farming in southern China back in the early 1990s. She has since led an international crusade aimed at closing down bear farms throughout Asia. Her efforts paid off when the Chinese government agreed to free 500 bears from some of the most notorious bear farms in the province of Sichuan. The first group of bears has since been taken to a rescue center run by the foundation where they are treated with a love and affection previously undreamed of.

It's likely to take a lot more international pressure, however, before the thousands of un-registered bears held in captivity throughout Asia are finally put out of their misery. In early 2002, the Vietnamese government, bowing to the demands of people like Robinson, passed a new wildlife law banning ownership of protected animals and effectively prohibiting all types of bear farming. But eighteen months later, there was little evidence that the industry is in decline. One bear farm even advertises its services in a newspaper published by the national police force. "Bear bile produced from live bear" reads the advertisement run in September 2003.

The farm in question is situated at the end of a narrow lane on the outskirts of Hanoi. It has twenty-five bears kept in the same trademark cages. Every Sunday morning at 8:30 a.m., first-time buyers come here to watch the animals being milked and to check that the bile is authentic. Outsiders are not welcome. "We only keep a small number of bears here in case we have problems with the police," admits Mr. Luong, the co-owner as he sips on a glass of rice wine mixed with bear bile.

△
The wholesale price of bear bile powder is around RMB4,000 (US $500) per kilogram. A whole gall bladder in South Korea can sell for about US $10,000, while in Japan the average price for a wild bear gall bladder is US $33 per gram.

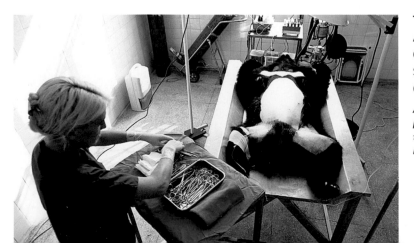

**The Animals Asia Foundation Centre Chengdu, Sichuan Province China**

*An asiatic black bear is prepeared for surgery to remove its gall bladder catheter.*

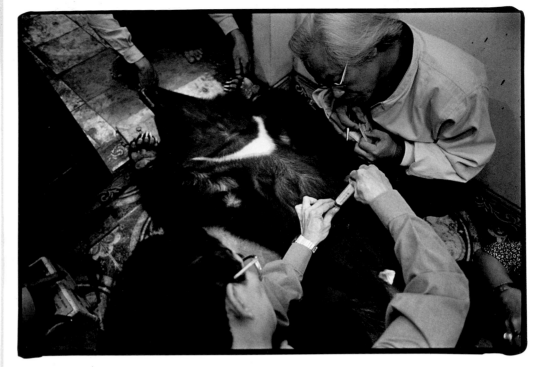

*At the bear farm in Hanoi, workers extract the bile from a bear's gall bladder before selling it for medicinal purposes.*

One bear farm even advertises its services in a newspaper published by the national police force. "Bear bile produced from live bear" reads the advertisement run in September 2003.

In this delightful old capital of lakes and tree-lined boulevards, there are other reasons for keeping bears. Back in 1996, Mr. Le Thanh, was working as a pediatrician in a local maternity clinic when he fell sick from a debilitating liver disease. He tried western medicine but to no avail. Given only weeks to live by doctors, a friend of his wife suggested that he try bear bile. The cure was so effective that Mr. Le Thanh gave up work and began farming and breeding bears for their bile, becoming one of the first commercial operators to do so. Today, he has six bears, which he keeps in cages on the second floor of his house on Ham Tho Quan Street. Every day he feeds them human placenta mixed with vegetable, bone, honey, and sticky rice—a recipe that he swears keeps them from getting fat. "The bile is better with this diet," he says.

In the years since Mr. Le Thanh started up his business, thousands of other Vietnamese have followed suit, part of an unstated government policy to use sustainable bear farming to create employment opportunities for rural communities. With so many suppliers, however, the price of bear bile has plunged in recent times, leading to a crisis among small-time owners who are finding it increasingly difficult to support their bears.

Unable to control the trade or to pay for the care of seized bears, the Vietnamese government is now talking of granting an amnesty to owners of bear farms, who register their bears with the authorities. Such an amnesty they say will ensure that further animals are not taken from the wild. But in Vietnam it is actions that speak louder than words. And so far there is little evidence of the will to change or to take criminal action against the people—mainly state officials, who perpetuate the illegal trade. ◤

◁ Medicinal uses for bear gall bladder first appeared in writing in the seventh century in the Chinese Materia Medica of medicinal properties.

# ALTERNATIVE MEDICINES

A large blue and red sign in Chinese script hangs above the dingy Hong Kong office of Dr. Lo Yan-wo, eminent doctor of traditional Chinese medicine and veteran member of the Hong Kong Herbal Association. Inside his tiny two-room clinic, the shelves are bursting with sachets of herbs, roots, twigs, and bottles of oil. But Dr. Lo is no local quack. With more than forty years of experience, he has successfully treated everything from flu to rheumatism and from kidney stones to cancer. What is more, he has done so using little more than rhubarb, dandelion, Japanese thistle, Madagascar periwinkle, and up to 100 other types of herbs and plants boiled together in different combinations.

That makes the frail-looking man something of a rarity in a region where wild animals have been used for centuries to treat a variety of ailments. But Dr. Lo, who learned his craft from his uncle in Guangdong province believes that the Chinese are changing their ways in the face of dwindling supplies and rising prices. "For thousands of years, Chinese herbalists have relied upon bear bile and other wildlife parts to remove poisonous substances from the body," he says. "Now there are many different combinations of herbs that can be administered in their place."

Dr. Lo's findings are backed by a growing body of scientific work. As far back as the 1950s, Japanese scientists discovered that ursodeoxycolic acid, the curative agent found in bear bile can be synthesized from pig, chicken, fish, and goat bile. Already, nearly 100 tons of synthesized bile are consumed every year in China, South Korea, and Japan to treat a host of different illnesses. Practitioners claim that the synthetic version is just as effective as the real thing and costs less than one tenth of the price.

Other medical discoveries have also revolutionized the way that scientists view the use of certain wildlife parts in traditional Chinese medicine. In the mid-1990s, Dr. Paul But Pui-hay, a respected professor at the Chinese University of Hong Kong, began analyzing the therapeutic effects of rhino horn. Using rats injected with turpentine to induce hyperthermia, Dr. But administered a range of different treatments made from combinations of rhino horn and herbs in order to observe the physical changes.

**Dr. Lo Lan Wo**

◁ Rhino horn has been used as an ingredient in traditional Asian medicine for 2,000 years. Ancient literary works and records as recent as the 16th century describe how cups made from rhino horn were used for detecting poisons. Just a few hundred years ago, some still held the belief that a poisonous liquid poured into the cup would bubble up. The cups may have succeeded occasionally in detecting strong alkaloid poisons, which would have reacted on contact with the keratin.

**Central Hong Kong**
*Good Spring Chinese*
*Herbal Pharmacy*

His results vindicated what the Chinese have argued for thousands of years: that rhino horn is effective in lowering feverish temperatures and counteracting toxins. Other findings were equally far-reaching. Tests revealed that buffalo horn can have a similar fever-reducing effect to rhino horn, although doses ten times higher may be sometimes required. In the most telling result of all, Dr. But's experiments confirmed that a combination of herbs taken without any type of horn could also lead to sharply lower temperatures.

In recent times, some of the biggest advances in the battle to save endangered wildlife species have come not from doctors of traditional Chinese medicine, but from mainstream pharmaceutical companies looking to exploit profitable new markets. The successful launch of a new generation of anti-impotence drugs like Viagra revealed massive demand for such products in the West. Now the hope is that they could take off in China, providing an alternative treatment for the tens of millions of Chinese who have previously relied on animal products to enhance their virility.

In Hong Kong, that process has already begun. According to local newspaper reports, sales of traditional sex tonics such as seal penises and ground reindeer antlers have seen a "modest but statistically significant" fall since the anti-impotence drug first became available. Two American biologists who surveyed Chinese medicine shops in the territory in early 2002 also found that men were turning less to traditional cures for impotence.

Test results reveal herbal combinations to be equally effective as ground rhino horn at reducing fever.

In Burma, elephant leg bones ground up and mixed with water are used to treat piles, whilst the lower section of the tail is hung in homes in the belief that it will bring success in business.

Realistically, however, it is going to take a lot more than Viagra or other types of herbal medicine to change a pattern of behavior which is still part of their culture for many elderly Chinese. In the more remote areas of the country where western medicine is still largely unknown or desperately expensive, a significant portion of the local population still believe that wildlife is the only effective cure for debilitating diseases such as encephalitis or intestinal cancer. And until a younger, better educated, and less superstitious generation grows up, even practitioners like Dr. Lo may face an uphill struggle in persuading users of traditional Chinese medicine around the world to change their ways.

"Are we winning the battle to save Asia's wildlife?" asks James Compton at TRAFFIC. "We have had some successes, but they are not enough. Unless more is done, ten years from now, we could lose a lot of species."

In Vietnam, turtle jelly, a gooey black substance, is popularly eaten as a snack to cure skin ailments and other ills and is also viewed as a symbol of good fortune.

**Hanoi, Vietnam**
**November, 2003**

*A traditional Chinese medicine supplier grinding and mixing various substances, including slivers of deer horn, as seen in the left portion of the image.*

ABOVE RIGHT

**Tachilek**
**Thailand Burma Border**
**September, 2003**

*A wildlife trader displays some of her wares. Tachilek is a major outlet and transit point for wildlife products.*

### China, Wushou

*Staff at the largest snake
repository sort snakes for
snake wine. More than one
million snakes are imported
to Wuzhou for export to the
kitchens of Hong Kong Macau,
and other regions in Asia.*

# THE UNDERGROUND CHANNELS

# TRAIL OF DEATH

India's border with Nepal cuts down through the stony plains of the southern *terai* past a series of spectacular mountain ridges, intersected to the east by rivers and lush tropical valleys. It is a landscape of breathtaking beauty stretching for almost 1,000 kilometers through scattered hills and tea plantations, rice fields, and an occasional forest. But this rugged border area has other less widely known distinctions. For it also contains one of Asia's biggest wildlife-smuggling routes and serves as a major transit point for illegal goods bound for Europe.

Every year, millions of dollars' worth of tiger bone, leopard skin, rhino horn, and ivory are smuggled out of India's north and northeastern provinces into remote districts of Nepal, from where they are transported further afield. Wildlife is not the only commodity that finds its way over these tortuous roads and mountain passes. Guns and drugs are also smuggled along this underground network that stretches from Mumbai (formerly Bombay) and Karachi to Hong Kong and the Middle East.

So porous is the India–Nepal border and so lax is the enforcement by the poorly paid guards stationed at its crossings, that for a bribe of around US $0.25 per day, local people and illegal laborers can walk from one country to the next virtually unchallenged. Once illegal goods reach the other side—hidden in rice sacks or occasionally carried on buffalo carts—local agents arrange to have them taken by courier on an overnight bus to the Nepalese capital, Kathmandu. From here they can be sent overland to China—or by air to virtually anywhere in the world.

In the early hours of 12 January 2000, police, acting on a tip-off, raided the Indian town of Khaga, which is a nine-hour drive from the border. Inside three illegal tanning factories, they discovered 18,000 leopard claws, 70 leopard skins, 4 tiger skins, and an assortment of other wildlife parts, conservatively valued at US $1 million. After an extensive search they also turned up another 175 kilograms of tiger bone and leopard bone on one of the sites,

**West Bengal
Calcutta
1985**

*The mother of Belinda Wright examines eight tiger skins and more than 136 leopard skins discovered inside a package.*

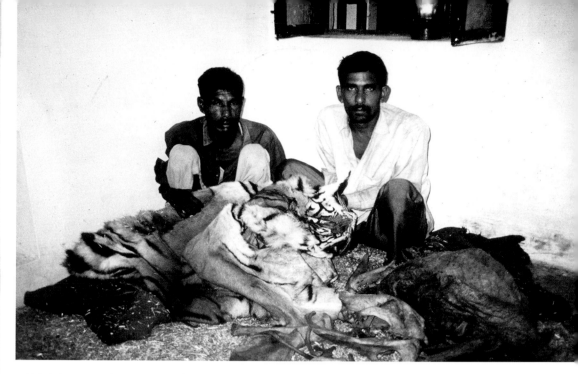

**1996**

*Two village poachers with tiger skins and bones held in a police station in the Indian town of Pallia.*

"When I started out in this business, most people involved in the trade were doing it as a full time profession," says Wright. "Today we are dealing with hard-core criminals involved in a whole range of illegal activities."

which is located only 200 meters from the local police station.

This was by far the largest seizure in India's recent history. Yet it marked the second major wildlife confiscation in less than a month. On 18 December, tax officials in Ghaziabad near Delhi had flagged down a vehicle that they suspected belonged to an international racket involved in smuggling illegal garments, a common activity in India's flourishing underground economy. What they discovered was far more serious. Concealed inside the vehicle and meticulously packaged in a consignment of cloth were fifty leopard skins, three tiger skins, and a handful of other skins ready to be shipped over the border like a batch of mass-produced textiles.

The third seizure was less dramatic. On 6 May 2000, fifty leopard skins were found in unclaimed railway parcels in the city of Haldwani. The parcels had been sent from the capital Delhi. Once again, they were due to be taken by truck to the India–Nepal border.

If anything could bring home the fact that India's wildlife laws were being broken with impunity this was it. Tests on the skins revealed that the majority of animals had been poisoned or electrocuted. A few may have been caught in traps and bludgeoned to death. But these staggering finds might be just the tip of the iceberg. Almost two years after the seizures, the illegal trade in wildlife between India and Nepal continues to flourish despite pledges by the two governments to clamp down on it.

From the great national parks of India, which are home to one of the largest and most diverse populations of wild animals in Asia, skins and parts are smuggled to Delhi, Calcutta, and the country's other teeming cities where most of the big traders are based. For generations families of skilled Indian taxidermists and traders have controlled the business. In the 1990s, growing profits started to attract a new generation of criminals. Much of the trade is now in the hands of Tibetans living in exile. One of them, Atuk Tsering Tamang from Humla in northeast Nepal, was arrested by Indian special task force police in early 2003. The others remain at large.

The underground channels have changed in other ways. As it has become tougher to move shipments, traffickers have diversified their routes and methods of concealment. On occasions, rhino horn and ivory pieces have been smuggled in tins of *ghee*, a type of salted butter. The *ghee* solidifies in cooler months making detection virtually impossible. Hollowed-out timber is also widely used. Increasingly, women and children act as "mules" to move smaller consignments.

Despite growing awareness of wildlife crime, most illegal animal parts reach their final destination. "India has never been very good at directing enforcement," says Belinda Wright, founder of the respected Wildlife Protection Society of India (WPSI), which is based in Delhi. Established in 1994, WPSI has files on more than 10,000 individuals suspected of being involved in the wildlife trade. "When I started out in this business, most people involved in the trade were doing it as a full time profession," says Wright, who is widely considered one of the country's leading wildlife investigators. "Today we are dealing with hard-core criminals involved in a whole range of illegal activities."

Better communications and new transportation networks are also opening up even the most remote areas of Asia offering new prospects for wildlife traffickers. Exploiting India's long coastline, smugglers traverse coastal routes between southern India and the United Arab Emirates in *dhows*, ferrying anything from ivory and falcons to gold and electronics. In Kashmir, tiger bone is bartered for the wool of the rare Tibetan antelope. Today, the illegal underground channels lead not only through the remote mountains of Nepal, but into neighboring Tibet, Burma, Pakistan and Bangladesh.

Like any criminal business, a handful of senior officials provide protection and take a hefty cut of the proceeds. Besides that, few people know what is going on in the remote border areas far from the government and administrative centers. In the case of wildlife, which was until recently openly traded, few people care. "Who is going to take notice of a few skins when there are big volumes of guns and drugs crossing over the border?" asks one enforcement official. 🐘

Who is going
to take notice
of a few skins
when there are
big volumes of
guns and drugs
crossing over
the border?

**Madhya Pradesh**
**1996**

*Police stand behind a haul*
*of seized leopard skins,*
*tiger skins, skulls, bones*
*and antlers.*

# THE HUNTERS OF ASSAM

On a moonlit night in January, Mohammed Khaleque and Mohammed Faizul leave the village of Kokowary, a sprawling settlement of tumbledown houses and festering sewers situated in the poverty-stricken plains of Assam in northeast India. Following a dirt track that leads towards the distant foothills, they make their way through the now deserted countryside to Pabitora Wildlife Sanctuary, home to seventy-five greater Asian one-horned rhinos.

In the shadowy grasslands on the fringes of the park, they are joined by a group of un-employed laborers from a neighboring village. The men work quietly, but with fierce concentration, always on the lookout for any sign of the park rangers who conduct night patrols and who shoot to kill. One of the villagers unwinds a coil of wire, which he attaches to the overhead power supply that runs along the park boundary. Supporting the wire on bamboo sticks, he strings it for almost a kilometer to an area the rhinos are known to frequent.

Rhinos are creatures of habit. Their eyesight is poor, but their sense of smell and hearing is acute. So the men wait downwind in silence. Finally, out of the darkness they glimpse the outline of a rhino lumbering down the trail toward them. Within seconds of touching the wire, the rhino is dead—electrocuted by 11 kilowatts, its head ripped asunder. For the poachers, however, the epi-sode also ends in tragedy. Two of the men touch the cable in error and die instantly. The others flee into the night but not before hacking off the valuable rhino horn with a hatchet.

Here, on the heavily populated plains of Assam, where informers are paid money to report such incidents, word of the killing travels fast. A day later, police from the Mayong district raid the village of Kokowary. They discover the rhino horn hidden in the back of a house. Two men are arrested on charges of assisting the poachers, and three others escape to neighboring states.

The underground channels, however, lead far beyond the poor villagers of Kokowary, who struggle to feed their families in whatever way they can. The real trade is darker, more invisible—extending its grasp with ruthless efficiency from the poachers to corrupt police and government officials and eventually via countless middlemen to the international smugglers who transport the rhino horns to their final destination.

Demand is the insidious force that drives the international

**Kaziranga National Park
Assam, India
May, 2003**

RIGHT AND BELOW
*Rangers patrolling on elephant.*

*Specially designed shotgun shells that are made to kill rhinos. In this case they are not being used to kill the rhino for its horn, but to protect the rangers from a charging rhino.*

গঁড়ে কেছো-
ময়ঁউ আপোনাৰদৰেই
সংকটাপন্ন
GREAT INDIAN ONE HORNED RHINOCEROS
I AM ENDANGERED
SO ARE YOU.

◁ Poachers cut overhead power cables and drape them over hundreds of yards of forest so that the live wires electrocute the animals. The hunters also dig traps and shoot the creatures before gouging out their horns.

**Pabitora Wildlife Sanctuary Assam, India 2003**

*A pair of great Asian one-horned rhinoceroses lie dead—electrocuted by poachers.*

trafficking of rhino horn. And with fewer than 3,000 Asian rhinos left in Southeast Asia, demand is at record highs. Since 1987 more than 600 rhinos have been shot, electrocuted, or poisoned in and around Assam's wildlife sanctuaries, despite the presence of some of the most dedicated rangers in the country. On the international black market, the rhino horns alone would fetch US $15 million. Local rangers joke that it's like guarding the crown jewels. In this case, however, the rhinos are uninsured, while the men who protect them are grossly underfunded and often outgunned.

Less than five kilometers as the crow flies from Kokowary, Mrigen Barua is on the radio, checking his outposts in Pabitora. A veteran ranger, he has spent the past twenty years battling to preserve one of the few remaining strongholds of the Asian rhino. His efforts very nearly cost him his life. The first time that poachers tried to kill him was in August 1998 when Mrigen was conducting a night patrol accompanied by three forest rangers. A group of men opened fire, sending the rangers scrambling for cover. In the subsequent shoot-out, one of the poachers was injured, but Mrigen escaped unscathed. On a second occasion in February 1999, a bullet smashed through the open window of Mrigen's vehicle as he was driving through the wildlife sanctuary, missing him by inches. "They tried to eliminate me because I was clamping down too heavily on poachers," he says, his voice trailing off into silence.

Staring out over the marshlands of Pabitora, now filled with crimson water lilies, spotted pond turtles and a profusion of waterfowl, it is hard to imagine that such events ever occurred. Cries of migratory birds fill the air as a fish-eating eagle swoops down on his prey, darting through the lush vegetation. A water monitor, the second largest lizard in the world, slithers through the glistening mud. In the distance, a herd of rhinos graze undisturbed in the late afternoon light.

Against all the odds, however, this stocky man with his neatly trimmed moustache and indomitable passion for wildlife, has successfully turned the tide at Pabitora. Over a five-year period, Mrigen has arrested dozens of poachers including Ab-

**Mai Sai/Tachilek**
**Thailand, Burma**
**September, 2003**

*In the Thai-Burma border town of Thachilek, a Asian rhino horn is put on display, the asking price is 8,000 USD. Tachilek is a major outlet and transit point for wildlife products.*

dul Kalam, believed to be one of the local masterminds behind the rhino killings. He has also confiscated large numbers of guns and ammunition. And with the assistance of Pradeep Nath, an incorruptible local police officer, he literally drove the poachers away.

It's a remarkable achievement, all the more so for the limited resources that park rangers have at their disposal and the disproportionate risks that these men take in the line of duty. It is also proof that close cooperation between rangers, conservationists and local communities can provide a real and lasting solution.

In neighboring Kaziranga National Park, home to the largest population of Asian rhinos in the world, similar collaboration has also yielded spectacular results. From rampant poaching in the early 1990s, the number of rhinos killed every year has fallen to a handful, thanks to rigorous enforcement, the use of paid informers, and the start up of a number of locally and internationally funded community projects. In the nearby towns and villages, families who once relied on illegal hunting for their income now sell fresh produce in local markets. The State Forestry Department has invested in new irrigation schemes. As many as 600 visitors now arrive in Kaziranga every day providing employment and a renewable source of income for the local people.

Success, however, has come at a price. Hunters who once targeted Pabitora and Kaziranga are looking further afield to other wildlife sanctuaries where rangers are not armed and where the risks of confrontation are lower. In the wildlife sanctuary of Manas, which straddles the India–Bhutan border, only a handful of rhinos remain out of a total of ninety-seven recorded less than a decade ago. Meanwhile, in Laokhawa Wildlife Sanctuary, a park that once boasted almost 5 percent of the world's rhino population, not one remains.

For Mrigen Barua and Pradeep Nath, who helped turn around the situation in Pabitora, there is also a sad ending. In late 2002 both men were transferred from their posts despite their unblemished record. Local officials claimed that it was a regular transfer, one of many carried out every year in Indian wildlife sanctuaries. But their removal was followed by a noticeable increase in poaching activities in the region.

Several months later, a far greater tragedy occurred. Nilom Bora, a courageous young wildlife conservationist who was instrumental in setting up a network of informers around the wildlife parks in Assam, was stabbed to death. His body was found lying on the side of the road, close to where he had been carrying out an undercover surveillance operation. He had suffered countless knife wounds to the head and chest, and had been dead for at least thirty-six hours when his body was recovered. Despite ongoing police investigations, his killers have not been apprehended. Nilom was just thirty years old when he died, the latest casualty of the war against poachers. ✦

Park rangers are the first to admit that until poverty is eradicated in the region or until the demand for wildlife is stamped out, the battle to save wildlife can never be won.

# THE KINGPINS OF DIMAPUR

In Nagaland, a remote province that sits astride the northeast Indian state of Assam and Burma, there is a popular local saying: the people from this region eat every thing with four legs except tables. Ferret badgers, civets, and geckos are all considered common fare and are openly sold in the sprawling open-air markets that are a feature of almost every town and village. So widespread is the consumption of animals that even dogs are conspicuous by their absence. Nagaland, however, is renowned for more than just its residents' appetite for exotic types of food. For it is here, in this narrow strip of mountainous territory, that some of the biggest wildlife traders are based.

"Hekta" and "Chettan" are two of the most prominent traders who operate out of Dimapur, the major commercial center of Nagaland. Well-known to the local authorities, they are believed to control as much as 80 percent of the market for rhino horn that comes out of northeast India and heads for Burma, Nepal, and Bhutan. So far, the traders have been able to avoid the occasional clamp down.

It's a situation that says as much about Nagaland's tumultuous and often violent history as it does about the government's reluctance to apprehend the traders. Closed off from the rest of the country for years because of intermittent fighting between the Indian army and separatist Naga guerillas, this mountainous region of 2 million inhabitants was until recently off-limits to outsiders. Even today, visitors to Nagaland need special passes. To avoid trouble, they need to keep a low profile.

The continuing unrest makes it relatively easy for criminal elements like Hekta and Chettan to operate virtually untouched by the authorities. Using aliases to conceal their real identity and communicating by mobile phones, they receive orders for rhino horns, ivory, and skins from buyers as far away as Hong Kong and the Middle East. They pass the orders on to local agents based in the nearby villages of Pietae and Golaghat, who then offer money to impoverished hunters. Working in small, organized groups, these men leave few traces of their own involvement. The poachers only deal with middlemen. The middlemen only know the names of two people higher up the chain of command.

The system thrives on complicity at the highest levels of local and regional government.

The system thrives on complicity at the highest levels of local and regional government. Big wildlife traders like Hekta receive protection from local politicians. The politicians in turn receive a share of the proceeds both from wildlife trafficking and from a host of other illegal businesses. The links between government officials and the criminal underworld generally extend even further. At election time, the kingpins will be called upon to coerce local voters into supporting these politicians. If necessary, they will turn to more violent means.

From Dimapur, the underground channels lead east to the state capital Kohima. It was here that the British and Indian army turned back the Japanese in one of the most important battles of the Second World War. From this pleasant hill station situated at an altitude of 1,495 meters, couriers transport illegal goods by bus to Silaguri, a city of 5 million people that in recent decades has emerged as a major center for trade and commerce. In this sprawling, dusty city, there is no shortage of people, many of them illegal immigrants, who are prepared to risk smuggling wildlife, guns, or drugs over the border into Nepal. A handful of agents based in Silaguri monitor the situation on the border, identifying routes and arranging transport for illicit goods. The police, who are poorly paid and often paid months in arrears, are generally only too happy to make some money and to turn a blind eye to such activities.

Outside of Dimapur, there is another route that is an increasingly popular alternative. If a rhino is killed in the western part of Kaziranga or Pabitora, the horn will be taken by bus to the town of Nagaon; from there it will be smuggled over the border into Bhutan. To avoid detection, couriers constantly shift bus routes and roads, passing the horn from one person to the next. After reaching Bhutan, the horn is sold to agents who will arrange to have it transported to Kathmandu. Or they may take one of hundreds of other routes that crisscross the region, far from the military checkpoints.

Like the black market trade in drugs, arms, or illegal immigrants, money is the oil that lubricates the wheels of the wildlife trade. A poacher who kills a rhino and removes its horn in the national parks of northeast India will receive anything from US $100 to US $400, although locals report that in some cases payment is simply a bicycle and a radio. By the time the horn is smuggled to the transit market in Dimapur, Silaguri, or Darjeeling, it could be worth anything up to US $18,000. When it reaches its final destination in Hong Kong or China, it will command a price of around US $38,000. Tiger bone can go for as much as US $500 per kilo in parts of Asia. Even an otter penis can sell for US $100.

With so much money at stake, it's no wonder that there are plenty of recruits looking for a one-way ticket to prosperity, or that when one is caught there are tens of thousands of other small-time traders prepared to take his place. Higher up the chain of command, the likelihood of

**Medan
Sumatra, Indonesia
October, 2003**

*A long tail Macaque
for sale at the bird market.*

Money is the oil
that lubricates
the wheels of the
wildlife trade.

being apprehended is virtually nil. The big wildlife traders can hire the best lawyers to get them off the hook or they simply abscond on bail. In India, however, it rarely goes that far. That's because there's almost always enough money to grease the palms of anyone who matters, including the police and the judges.

"It can take years to bring an illegal trader to court," says Ashok Kumar, a veteran investigator, who works as an advisor to the Wildlife Trust of India. "Under current laws, these criminals cannot be charged unless they are physically caught in possession of illegal wildlife."

On 29 April 2004, Sansar Chand, one of India's most notorious wildlife traders, was sentenced to five years in jail on charges relating to the illegal possession of leopard skins. Conservationists hailed the conviction as a turning point in the country's struggle to enforce the Wildlife Protection Act. Within a month, however, Chand, was released from prison on a technicality.

Meanwhile dealers in neighboring countries make few pretenses about where their most valuable wildlife originates. Unpacking a carton labeled as toilets, Mr. Lu, a Burmese wildlife trader in the scruffy border town of Tachilek, produces a collection of the finest quality tiger and leopard skins together with a set of tiger's teeth, which he guarantees will bring good luck. "All our best skins come from India," he says. "These arrived just this morning. There are plenty more where they came from."

Ironically, the official border post manned by Thai and Burmese police lies less than 100 meters from Mr. Lu's shop. Not that it presents any great obstacle for a resourceful trader. "You want to take the skins back to Thailand?" he says. "I will arrange for somebody to carry them over. No problem." ➹

**Guwahati, Assam, India, 2003**

*Two men selling rhino horn for medicinal purposes, in front of a Guwahati mosque.*

**Birganj, Nepal/Indian Border, January, 2004**

*A sign welcoming travelers to Nepal, this is the major crossing point in Nepal for the smuggling of wildlife into Nepal and India.*

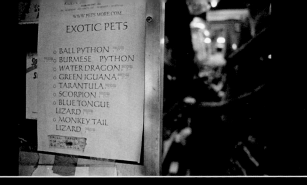

# The Internet Trader

In a dimly lit office in the Malaysian capital Kuala Lumpur, Chris Shepherd is surfing the Internet in search of rare and exotic animals. Names of pet shops flash up on the screen. Some sell cats and dogs; others offer more interesting possibilities. Scrolling down lists of dealers, it does not take long to find what he is looking for. On one website, finest quality pythons from Indonesia are for sale; on another, slithering iguanas and rare butterflies.

And that's just the small stuff. To find the more valuable species, like rare Burmese star tortoises (U.S.$13,000 per pair) or Timor monitors, involves more time and effort. It may take several hours or days of negotiating in an Internet chat room followed by a covert phone conversation and a faxed message of confirmation. For the dedicated buyer of endangered species, however, there are few real obstacles.

"All the dealers claim that they breed the animals themselves," says Shepherd, a veteran wildlife investigator who works for TRAFFIC, an organization that monitors the wildlife trade. In many cases, it's an entirely legal occupation. But there are no shortage of illegal operators who obtain their animals from the wild.

The Internet has revolutionized international trafficking of rare and endangered species like nothing before. In the days before dealers went high tech, purchasing illegal animals was a long drawn-out affair. Now every type of exotic creature is just a click away, transforming cyberspace into a gigantic animal wildlife supermarket. Better still for dealers, it's safe and anonymous.

Estimating the size of the illegal trade is almost impossible. However there's little doubt about one thing: trading over the Internet is the fastest growing area of wildlife crime. Live reptiles and traditional Chinese medicine containing illegal wildlife parts are commonly sold online throughout Europe and the U.S. Items ranging from tiger skins to the shell of the critically endangered hawksbill turtle even appear occasionally on the world's biggest online auction house, eBay. Meanwhile, in countries like Malaysia, Indonesia, and Singapore, it is believed to be a virtual free-for-all.

Once a deal has been reached and a money transfer arranged, the animals will probably be sent by courier, packed in specially perforated boxes. Smart dealers obtain real or phony permits saying that the animals are captive bred and therefore legal. Or they may hide the animals deep inside crates of common species. These days, to the alarm of postal workers, growing numbers of snakes and other small reptiles are sent by mail.

If it is so easy to order illegal wildlife, why doesn't someone stop it? For a start, most enforcement agencies do not have the time or expertise to check up on the tens of thousands of cross-border transactions that take place every day. Furthermore, there are enough loopholes in most country's wildlife laws for an elephant to jump through.

What is not available on the Internet is generally advertised by word of mouth or through networks of wildlife collectors who distribute price lists among themselves and exchange information at international forums. In the U.S. alone, about 400 wild- pet and breeding fairs are held around the country every year. Many of the big events, like the Florida International Reptile Expo in Orlando attract the big international wildlife dealers who go to enlarge their circle of contacts. Once again, it's all aboveboard except that most of the illegal deals are arranged on the sidelines.

As fast as wildlife investigators like Shepherd can gather information about the trade, dealers find alternative ways to circumvent the laws. "Wildlife dealers use fake names and log in from Internet cafes," he says. "These people know the laws. They attend CITES conferences and they exploit the loopholes."

# HIMALAYAN NETWORKS

If you follow the illegal wildlife channels from India through to China, across the rugged foothills of the Himalayas, at some stage you are bound to end up in Nepal. Buttressed between its two giant neighbors and with a border that stretches for 2,500 kilometers, this remote and mountainous kingdom has long included part of the old salt route that lured traders over its icy passes with the promise of undreamed of wealth. Today, however, Nepal has fallen on hard times. Torn apart by a bloody civil war that has killed thousands, the kingdom has been largely deprived of the tourist revenues that were once its economy's lifeblood. As a result, Kathmandu, the capital city, is fast becoming a modern-day Casablanca, teeming with wildlife traffickers, drug smugglers, gunrunners, and government informers who lurk in its thriving underworld.

To the extent that it is visible, the wildlife trade is situated in the Thamel and Patan districts, where for decades backpackers and tourists have stayed en route for treks to the Himalayas. Along the narrow streets, now clogged with half-empty hotels and souvenir shops, vendors still tout hippy waistcoats, fake CDs and cheap wooden elephants. But as tourist dollars have dwindled the trade has shifted to other more lucrative areas of business.

Inquiries about illegal wildlife products are at first met with blank stares and denials. Over glasses of Assam tea and pleasantries exchanged in the back of shops, however, most owners soon warm to the idea of making a quick profit. Within hours of arriving in Thamel, a flurry of phone calls leads to offers of *shathoosh*, the highly prized wool extracted from the throat and underbelly of the endangered chiru, gunned down by the thousands on the icy slopes of Tibet. Purchased here in the underground markets of Kathmandu for US $1,000, the same shawl can be sold in Europe or the U.S. for fifteen times that amount. Ivory trinkets, python skin handbags, and coats made from leopard skin are also for sale, warehoused in other parts of town to avoid unwanted attention.

It's a common enough story in this picturesque capital of temples and golden pagodas. A short distance from Thamel in the district known as Bouddha, vendors openly sell birds such as golden parakeets and red muniyas despite regulations banning the trade and transit of wildlife.

For every wildlife bust that takes place in Asia, law enforcement agencies fear that probably around ten times that amount gets through.

**Chitwan National Park
Sauraha, Nepal
January, 2004**

*A small group of Royal
Nepalese solders patrolling on
elephant at daybreak.*

The vendors also take orders for rarer species such as hornbills and falcons, kept out of sight to avoid unwelcome inquiries. Smuggled over the border by the thousand from the town of Patna in northwest India, the birds are often flown via Hong Kong to Pakistan. There collectors snap them up or mix them in with non-endangered bird species, then send them to Europe.

In Kathmandu's closely-knit underground network, the channels for wildlife operate largely by word of mouth. Bouchon, a friendly Nepali in his late thirties, works in an antique shop situated close to the Boudhanath Stupa, one of the city's most revered and ancient shrines. He sells finely woven carpets, authentic Tibetan furniture, and Himalayan tribal art. He also acts as a conduit for less legal types of business. Asked if he knows where to buy chests covered in tiger skin, Bouchon initially shrugs his shoulders and denies any knowledge. But after an hour of gentle coaxing, he admits that he has a friend who may be of assistance.

Two phone calls later a Tibetan trader built like a colossus leads the way down a narrow alleyway to an unmarked garage, its door firmly bolted with a brand new padlock. Inside the dimly lit garage, an Aladdin's cave of wildlife items is stacked up to the ceiling: wooden chests covered with tiger skin; antique boxes wrapped in leopard skin; pieces of finely carved furniture cloaked in snow leopard skin. Prices start at just US $1,000 apiece, with a special discount for bulk orders. And transport is not a problem. To conceal the skins from the prying eyes of customs officials, leather is sewn around the boxes prior to shipment. "Nobody will ever know what is inside," says Bouchon. And so far none of his clients have been stopped.

Bouchon's excellent contacts in the export business also ensure that there will be no difficulty getting the chests out of Tribhuwan Airport, Nepal's only international airport and the most common exit point for wildlife sent illegally to Europe, the Middle East, and other Asian markets. Most customs officials can't tell the difference between an endangered animal and a legal export, says Bouchon. Those that can are generally persuaded to look the other way.

Like the illegal trafficking of "blood diamonds" in Angola or the black market trade in timber and narcotics in Burma, it's political conflict that has helped fuel the dizzy rise of wildlife trafficking here in Nepal. In the remote western part of the country, Maoist rebels battling for a communist republic are

**Chitwan National Park
January, 2004**

*At the Bharatpur barracks a group of Royal Forestry Department Officers display seized tiger and snow leopards skins. The stockpile is five years old and the value is an estimated US $750,000.*

blamed for a spate of rhino killings that have shocked this country, which is already hardened by years of war. In a matter of weeks twenty rhinos were killed and their horns probably bartered for weapons on the Chinese border.

For those men who are caught, there is little mercy. In the town of Kasara, on the southern fringes of the Royal Chitwan National Park, there is a military jail used to temporarily lock up poachers. It's dark and dingy and reeks of human excrement. Half a dozen men believed to be part of a local poaching gang are held under guard behind barbed wire fences. Unwashed and frightened looking, they were picked up two weeks earlier during one of the regular night patrols. But they have not yet

The Royal Chitwan National Park, 150 miles southwest of Kathmandu, Nepal, has one of the largest number of tigers and rhinos in the world, and, consequently, is witness to the most instances of poaching. Last year alone, 100 poachers in this region were arrested.

been formally charged with poaching offenses and they were not found in possession of wildlife.

The web of intrigue that surrounds the wildlife trade in Nepal extends far beyond the armed rebels, international traffickers, and small-time poachers that flourish in this increasingly lawless kingdom. Back in 1992, a young reporter by the name of Mangal Man Shakya was working on a story about the rhino trade when he came across a stunning discovery. A trust operated by the Nepalese Royal family was giving pairs of live rhinos to zoos in various foreign countries in exchange for US $250,000 donations. The money was placed in a numbered bank account at Grindlays Bank (now Standard Chartered Bank) and not even the Department of National Parks and Wildlife Conservation knew of its existence. Questions remain about whether the money was a gift or a cover up for a major incident of wildlife trafficking and about why nobody outside the trust appeared to be aware of the payment.

**Kolkata, India**
**May, 2003**

*Inside one the oldest gunsmith shops in India; the shop has been in the same family for five generations. It was the first port of call when the "Great White Hunters" from England hit the shores of India.*

On a Sunday afternoon in March, Shakya is seated in one of the many teahouses scattered around the Thamel district of Kathmandu. A reporter turned wildlife investigator, this generous and warm-hearted man has done much to bring the plight of the country's wildlife to the attention of both the government and conservationists. On one of his most recent trips, Shakya spent thirty days on the Tibetan border as part of a team sent in to track down hunters of the rare Tibetan antelope. Since then Shakya, who is now chairman of the Wildlife Watch Group, has traveled all around the region in a bid to pressure governments to take action to stem the trade. "How is it that the trade is so large and the response so small?" he says without so much as a note of bitterness in his voice.

Few Nepalese believe that the situation will change any time soon. More money put aside for wildlife enforcement means fewer funds to fight the rebels and fewer kickbacks for the military and provincial authorities who take a cut from the black market trade. And when corruption goes all the way to the top, there is nobody left to set an example. ♠

# GOING FOR A SONG

**The bird market on Jalan Bintang in the Indonesian city of Medan is a must-see spot for tourists. On almost any day, it bristles with cages containing red- and yellow-crested parrots, rare cockatoos, and kingfishers—going almost for a song. Fifteen years ago, there were about a dozen shops selling exotic birds and pets in this ugly, traffic-choked city. Now there are close to forty and business is booming thanks to an influx of buyers not only from Indonesia, but from as far away as the Netherlands—lured by the promise of rare and often illegal birds at bargain prices.**

"Tony" is one of the major bird dealers on Jalan Bintang. His crowded two-storied shophouse openly sells blue and gold macaws from Brazil for around US $2,000, despite the fact that they are endangered. He also has a pair of African gray parrots from Tanzania with a price tag of US $1,200, although you can bargain the price down by at least a quarter. "The birds are expensive because they are flown in via Singapore and Kuala Lumpur," admits Tony's assistant, who recommends a pair of endangered Bali birds, probably trapped in one of the country's national parks. In the unlikely event that the police or forestry officials decide to raid Jalan Bintang, Tony is normally tipped off in advance.

Less than fifty meters away from Tony's shop, is another of the well-known dealers in Medan. "Wirun," an Indonesian of Chinese descent, sells rare birds as well as long-tailed macaques and leopard cats that he keeps in small cages in front of the shop. He's been in the business for at least a decade. He also has friends in high places, which is a distinct advantage when it comes to buying and selling protected animals or obtaining permits for transporting them out of the country.

But the most powerful man of all when it comes to trading illegal wildlife in Medan is "Nasi." He used to work in a bird shop on Jalan Bintang, but has since found a more lucrative career by going freelance. Many dealers claim to have Nasi's phone number. When they need anything from an orangutan (with its teeth ripped out so owners and handlers don't get bitten) to a Sumatran tiger, they simply phone in the order.

And Nasi gets a lot of calls. If Britain is famous for its love of dogs, Indonesia has developed a reputation for its national obsession with birds. A dazzling array of bird markets spans the country's far-flung islands and cities trying to satisfy the craving of the its 220 million people. Word on the

**Medan, Indonesia
October, 2003**

*'Billy,' a major bird dealer in the Medan market.*

In the far
flung islands
of Indonesia,
pregnant women
eat the Black-
naped oriole in
the belief that it
will make their
babies beautiful.

street has it that demand for protected birds and animals has never been higher. Indeed, dealers on Jalan Bintang often use the fact that a bird is illegal as a major selling point.

Every year as many as 300 bird species are bought and sold in Medan, equivalent to tens of thousands of birds. Far from being the largest market in the country, Jalan Bintang is easily eclipsed by Surabaya, Yogyakarta, and the capital Jakarta. So prevalent is the trade in Jakarta's Pramuka Market that the authorities regularly put up posters warning against the illegal sale of wildlife and include the photographs and names of protected birds of prey. Dealers take no notice and simply scrawl the price of each bird below its photograph.

"Indonesia is one of the biggest markets for exotic pet birds anywhere in the world," says Chris Shepherd at the monitoring group TRAFFIC, which carried out a three-year investigation on the bird trade in Jalan Bintang. "As the numbers of birds become depleted here, they ship them in from outside the region."

At dusk on the island of Papua in the remote eastern part of the country, the parrot catchers of Kabara are already hard at work. Often as many as fifty of them will head into the forests, for as long as three days at a time, in search of rare birds from which they can earn themselves and their family a decent living. These experienced catchers trap birds by smearing branches with a gum they make from the forest's breadfruit tree. When the bird catchers see a parrot flying overhead, they beat a caged bird until its cries attract the passing creature. As soon as the parrot alights, its legs stick to the branch. Normally the birds are easily released, but occasionally their legs will snap as they're being removed, rendering them valueless to the villagers. As a result, growing numbers of

Pramuka Market in Jakarta, Indonesia sells about 30,000 birds a month or more than 300,000 birds a year.

**October, 2003**

*One of the many bird shops
in the bird market, Medan.*

bird catchers now use nylon nets and snares, which they place along the usual bird-passing areas.

On the first stage of their journey, these vulnerable creatures are taken to the port of Sorong, where they are sold to local traders. Eventually the birds are sent by private commercial ships or by air to Maluku or Java, using suppliers like Usahu Baru, Firma Hasco, or C.V. Rahmat. They may end up being sold in Pramuka Market, which is probably the biggest bird market in Asia, or they may continue their journey to Jalan Bintang in Medan. Nowadays plenty find their way to pet shops in neighboring countries like Singapore or Malaysia, or even to the Middle East, where birds command especially high prices. Many privately owned zoos in both Indonesia and Malaysia act as laundering centers, ordering birds which are sold on at a hefty profit.

That's when good connections with Department of Forestry officials can pay off handsomely. Every year, the department issues trapping quotas on birds for the domestic and export market. Often the permits are issued even when there are no quotas or when quotas have been exceeded. In the case of protected birds, plenty of other loopholes exist to facilitate the trade—aided by a well-greased palm and the fact that few people can tell the difference between species.

"Transporting birds by plane is the easy part," says Shepherd, who has seen crate-loads of birds put onto flights with no papers at all. "Occasionally the dealers simply fill in official documents and call them rare pigeons."

Airlines like Bouraq, Merpati, or Malaysian Airlines earn big money by accepting consignments of birds and turtles as cargo. In some cases, transportation permits accompany the shipments, so on paper everything appears aboveboard. However many of the birds declared as farmed have actually been taken from the wild. Others are mislabeled or lack the necessary quarantine documents.

Higher up Indonesia's echelons of power, the illegal trade is even more rampant. Investigations undertaken by ProFauna Indonesia, a local conservation organization, have uncovered evidence of large numbers of rare parrots being shipped into the big cities by Indonesian soldiers. The men buy the birds at the end of their tour of duty in order to supplement their meager wages, which are almost never paid in full. Rarely does anyone stop them.

As is the case with the Sumatran tiger and the fast-disappearing Sumatran orangutan, a bird's rarity drives up its price. This makes the most prized species harder to find, and forces wildlife traders like Tony to sell more common birds. As these also disappear, he will move to a new line of stock. But one day the songbirds will all be gone and the forests will be silent. ✒

FOLLOWING PAGE
*The northern border town of
Tachilek between Thailand and
Burma. Thailand is on the left,
Burma on the right.*

# BORDERLANDS

The large airfreight consignment did not look out of place among the thousands of other containers piled up inside Hanoi's Noi Bai International Airport. The 240 wooden cargo cases had been flown in that morning from Malaysia and were addressed to the Viet Thai company in Hanoi. When customs officials opened the consignment, they found more than 600 pangolins, a protected species commonly known as the anteater, which is popular for its scales and meat. The combined street value of the haul was put in excess of US $20,000.

On this occasion, police decided to investigate. But their questions led to an almost laughable story. The Vietnamese importer claimed that the company had ordered common turtles, which are not subject to trade restrictions, and refused to take responsibility for the illegal consignment. The Malaysian shipper alleged that the wrong batch of animals had been sent in error. Meanwhile, the pangolins were taken to a wildlife rescue center outside Hanoi, where 200 of them promptly died after being fed a diet of eggs, rice, and broth. Several weeks later, the remaining pangolins were incinerated. It was, said the authorities, necessary to destroy them in order to prevent the spread of disease.

Vietnam is one of the biggest wildlife transit markets in the whole of Asia. From here, the smuggling routes invariably lead to China. After leaving the capital Hanoi, the wildlife is driven north through the fertile plains of the Red River delta. Eventually, the animals pass through the spectacularly mountainous Chi Lang Pass before descending into the border province of Lang Son.

The local people have an expression to describe this wild and sparsely populated region. They call it *lam luat*, which means "to make your own law." In 1979, it was the scene of intense fighting when the Chinese invaded and partially destroyed the provincial capital. But peace has bought handsome dividends. Today, trade is the lifeblood of Lang Son and the surrounding region. And like a gigantic funnel, it channels wildlife and other illegal goods into the world's most populous nation.

A few buildings and a customs outpost are all that mark the official border post near Dong Dang, in the far north of Lang Son. A profusion of glistening vegetation clings to the surrounding hills, now the preserve of smugglers and armed soldiers who guard this volatile and heavily fortified area. For much of the day, trucks piled high with timber products and vegetables line up outside a handful of border checkpoints. After a perfunctory search, they continue their journey to the Chinese towns of Pinxiang and Nanning.

**Bangkok International Airport December, 2003**

*A shipment of Pangolins that were intercepted at Bangkok's international airport as part of a crackdown on wildlife trafficking. A customs official said this latest haul was packed in boxes marked as containing turtles. "We found them in 102 boxes originating from Kuala Lumpur and transiting here on their way to Vientiane," he said.*

**Map of Hanoi Smuggling Route**

*Vietnam's smuggling superhighway, from Hanoi through the Lang Son border province into China.*

More than five thousand pangolins were seized by Thai authorities in 2003 and were presumed to be bound for China via Laos, Vietnam and Cambodia where they are also consumed. Pangolin blood is eaten in the belief that it helps keep the body warm and enhances sexual performance.

At nighttime, however, the region takes on a different guise. From villages scattered along the border, pangolins, macaques, rare turtles, and other wild animals that have been temporarily warehoused are collected by couriers on motorcycles and taken to a prearranged location. Once the animals have been placed into larger consignments, they are driven to Dong Dang and other unofficial crossings before being carried illegally into China by groups of porters. On the far side of the border, the wildlife is loaded back into trucks and sold to traders in the local markets. The traders, in turn, sell the animals to other dealers, fanning them out throughout this increasingly prosperous country.

Although figures for the trade are notoriously unreliable, it is estimated that at least two or three tons of illegal wildlife pass over Vietnam's border into China every day, driven by sharply higher prices. With demand for wild meat outstripping supply, China is even importing live dogs and domestic cats. But the black market trade offers lucrative returns in both directions. From China, electronic goods and automobile parts are smuggled back into Vietnam. The border guards take a cut both ways, as do badly paid local government officials. "Nothing on the border happens without the knowledge of the border police," says Vu Ngoc Thanh, a primatologist and Museum Director at Vietnam's National University. "If these men stop the illegal trade, they will end up with empty stomachs."

Occasionally, however, an order does come down from the top that sends tremors through the smuggling syndicates and racketeers that flourish in this rugged border region. In June 2002, Vietnamese police arrested Dang Xuan Thanh, who together with his three brothers was believed to be responsible for up to 95 percent of the goods smuggled into Lang Son. Nearly twenty-five tons of electrical goods, automobile parts, and other black market goods were discovered in a cave used by Thanh and more than 100 associates. While the crackdown caused a temporary setback, villagers in Dong Dang claim that the nocturnal trade still continues, although at more subdued levels.

Nowadays, to avoid roadblocks and stricter enforcement at airports, traders are turning to more ingenious methods of smuggling. Tourist buses, military vehicles and ambulances are all used to transport illegal shipments. On one occasion, police found two live bears and more than 200 kilograms of protected wildlife hidden inside a prison truck in the central province of Nghe An. Even the old express train that shunts twice daily from Hanoi to Dong Dang is a popular channel for small consignments of wildlife. Traders conceal goods in secret compartments, often with the knowledge of railway officials. Sometimes the wildlife will ride in the engine car with the driver.

If it were not for the fact that such mass exploitation is driving many species to the brink of extinction, the situation would appear almost comical. But the tragedy in Vietnam is especially poignant. Having survived American carpet bombing and the devastation caused by aerial spraying of Agent Orange and other toxic defoliants, the country's fragile ecosystem is literally being traded into

"Nothing on the border happens without the knowledge of the border police," says Vu Ngoc Thanh, a primatologist and Museum Director at Vietnam's National University. "If these men stop the illegal trade, they will end up with empty stomachs."

**Mong La, Wa State**
**Burma**

*Pangolins lie curled as buyers inspect them. Mong La represents a virtual free zone in terms of wildlife trade, with high volumes of endangered animals being consumed on a regular basis.*

Seven species of pangolins are included in the single family Manidae, confined to the warmer parts of Asia and Africa, south of Sahara. Hunting and habitat destruction have made these strangely scaled mammals one of the most endangered groups in the world.

oblivion. At least a dozen large mammals and birds have gone extinct since the end of the Indochina war including the Sumatran rhino, the kouprey and the Eld's deer. "In Vietnam we estimate that there are only about twenty or thirty tigers left in the wild," says Vu Ngoc Thanh. "Soon they will be extinct."

Inside Thanh's office in a rambling colonial-style building off Hanoi's Nguyen Trai Road is the skeleton of a tiger. The skeleton had previously been on display in one of the adjacent exhibition rooms alongside specimens of other wild animals. Several years earlier, a visitor had attempted to steal the tiger's teeth, which are believed to bring luck, so staff were forced to move it to a safer location. "Every animal part in Vietnam has value," says Thanh, a small, ebullient man, shrugging his shoulders in resignation.

It's a telling reminder of what conservationists are up against if they are to turn back the tide of extinction. The repercussions of this obsession with wildlife, however, go far beyond Vietnam's own borders. Because the country has emptied most of its own countryside of wildlife, traders are being forced to acquire birds and animals from more distant areas. In Vinh, a provincial town in the northern region, dead tigers smuggled in from Laos are priced at US $15,000. The animal's bones are cooked for seven days and seven nights until they turn to paste and then sold through a network of local dealers for medicinal use. Wildlife is also smuggled into Vietnam from Cambodia along the remote border crossing at Ratanakiri province or by plane and boat from Singapore, Malaysia, Thailand, and Indonesia.

Once simply a transit market, Vietnam is also rapidly emerging as a major wildlife consumer. In almost every town and city, people order snakes, freshwater turtles, and lizards with barely a second thought. As economic liberalization brings new prosperity to the people of Vietnam, demand has increased. "About 90 percent of Vietnam's population are potential consumers of wildlife," says Trinh Le Nguyen of Education for Nature, an organization that seeks to inform local people about the environmental damage caused by the trade. "Unless we can do more to educate them, they will use their money to buy animals."

In January 2003, government officials finally did something to educate the local population. They arrested Vo Thanh Long, a former director of the Ho Chi Minh City Department of Industry, for poaching an endangered ox from an army-controlled nature reserve. Thanh Long was subsequently sentenced to three years in jail. Two other accomplices were handed down shorter prison sentences. The case was the first time that a high-ranking government official had faced such a penalty. "We are trying to stop the wildlife trade," says Vo Quay, one of the country's most respected conservationists, who is now advising the government. "But it's not easy." 🦡

# END OF THE ROAD

In early 2003, shortly after the start of the Chinese Year of the Goat, a highly inauspicious event occurred in southern China. Thousands of police descended on the notorious wildlife markets in Guangzhou province, randomly confiscating animals in a series of pre-dawn raids almost unheard of since the days when Chairman Mao outlawed sparrows and rats. The roundup reached a peak when large numbers of civets and raccoon dogs were seized outside Guangzhou's main airport and taken away in trucks to be put in isolation or drowned in chemical disinfectant. It was as if the fury of the gods had finally come to rest on the plunderers of the wild and the purveyors of farm-bred animals.

But the clampdown had nothing to do with saving wildlife. In the proceeding weeks, hundreds of people had died of a mysterious disease whose flu-like symptoms included coughing and a high fever. Known as Severe Acute Respiratory Syndrome or SARS, the disease struck with sudden virulence, sending many patients into a coma from which they failed to recover and triggering panic in cities around the globe.

Laboratory tests undertaken by Chinese microbiologists seeking the origins of the disease revealed the chilling possibility that the virus may have jumped to humans from a small weasel-like creature known as the masked palm civet. Overnight, the Chinese moved to ban wildlife in markets throughout the country. Suddenly it looked like the deadly disease might bring about what conservationists had wanted for years: an end to the worldwide trade in wild meat.

Within months, however, the diminutive cat-like creature responsible for the chaos was back on sale, its delicate meat touted once again for its special medicinal qualities and as a defense against the cold. "Many Chinese people still believe in the benefits of consuming wildlife," says Endi Zhang at the Wildlife Conservation Society in Shanghai. "When it is no longer openly available, it simply goes underground."

For anyone following the wildlife trafficking routes of Asia, China

**Guangzhou Southern China**

*Loading and unloading at the market.*

**Guangzhou**

*A market trader prepares food next to her raccoon dogs at the Xin Yuan market. Such markets have been identified by health authorities as a likely breeding ground for deadly viruses such as SARS.*

is the last stop on the road to extinction. Like a giant octopus, with long tentacles extending far into south and southeast Asia, China once stockpiled large amounts of tiger bone and rhino horn to supply its burgeoning market for traditional medicine. Nowadays that supply and much of its own wildlife have virtually dried up, forcing China to smuggle in animals from elsewhere in Asia. Between 1990 and 1992, 71 tons of tiger products—including 57,000 bottles of tiger wine and 247,000 containers of tiger derivatives—were traded between China and neighboring countries. That could amount to as much as 10 percent of the world's remaining population of tigers. Since then, no official statistics have been published.

As China has faced growing international criticism over its role in the international wildlife trade, however, its authorities have begun to clamp down on the most visible aspects of the trade. As a result, wildlife smuggling has become more organized and less open, largely conducted outside the major cities and concentrated in the hands of traders who ply the remote border areas that are virtually impossible to police.

Nothing marks the border between China and Burma near the remote town of Ruili except a small barbed-wire fence that parallels the road a short distance from the official crossing at Jiegao. In places, the wire has been pushed aside, leaving just enough space for a person to slide underneath. Smugglers' cargoes vary. Under cover of darkness they sometimes transport amphetamines that are

illegally manufactured inside Burma's notorious "Golden Triangle." At other times they carry wild animals, illegal immigrants, or counterfeit goods.

Less than a kilometer from this desolate spot, on the banks of the Ruili River, the cross-border trade is even more open. Unguarded by any customs outpost, porters from the village of Mensha load and unload boats that scurry across the river piled high with sacks of corn, illegal motorcycle components, and other unidentifiable goods. The men use mobile phones, the modern weapon of all smugglers, to communicate with their Burmese counterparts on the far bank of the river. As dusk falls, however, they grow unhappy at the presence of strangers. Maybe it was the imminent arrival of a consignment of amphetamines that made them restless or maybe the simple fear of the unknown. "There are many robbers and bad people in this area who deal in drugs," says one of the porters. "You must go."

In reality, it's probably small volumes of illicit goods that find their way over the river at Mensha. But further south in the village of Meng Jun, there is another crossing for illegal goods, and further along the banks of the river, there are tens or maybe hundreds more crossings. Added together they amount to huge profits for the black market. A few years back, Chinese police seized 2,000 wild animal skins from a single factory in Ruili. The skins, together with a collection of monkey heads and bear paws, had been smuggled in from Burma and were being sent by mail to buyers all over China.

In Ruili's jade market, a narrow concourse of crowded alleyways where precious stones can fetch up to US $100,000 apiece, Yang Wei, a gem trader with three passports and an intricate network of contacts makes few pretenses about what comes over the border. "You can buy tiger, live bears, everything," he says, puffing away on a succession of local cigarettes. A kilo of heroin smuggled in from Burma sells for US $6,000. Business has been good in recent years with most contraband finding its way north before it's taken into Kazakhstan and then dispatched to Russia and Europe. In 2002 alone, police and customs officials seized a total of nine tons of heroin in China with a street value in excess of US $55 million.

North of Ruili, a spectacular road snakes its way up into the mountains over the snow-clad pass at 4,000 meters before descending in to the town of Pian Ma. It's a grueling drive, made all the more treacherous by sudden snowstorms or landslides. Every day, hundreds of logging trucks drive through the border checkpoint at Pian Ma, transporting timber from the forests in Burma. The

**Mai Sai/Tachilek
Burma, Thailand
September, 2003**

LEFT ABOVE
*A shophouse displaying wildlife products for sale in the Thai-Burma border town of Thachilek. Tachilek is a major outlet and transit point for wildlife products.*

RIGHT ABOVE
*A wildlife trader displays some of his wares.*

**Xin Yuan Market Guangzhou**

*Wildlife markets are ready-made breeding grounds for a host of diseases. Here a shopkeeper reads about SARS connection to wildlife trade.*

truckers also bring animals to earn extra money. A few years ago, most types of wild animal were openly sold in Pian Ma. Now they are harder to come by. "Everyone knows the wildlife trade is illegal and that you will get in trouble with the police," says the owner of the Chong Cheng City restaurant. "If you want to buy wildlife you should go to Burma."

Inquiries around town uncover a similar story. But while more severe penalties and high-profile crackdowns have removed the wildlife trade from public view, they have failed to stop it. In late 2003, Chinese police manning a checkpoint in Sansan, a small township in southwest Tibet, received a tip-off about a major wildlife consignment en route to Lhasa. When police stopped a vehicle suspected of carrying the illicit goods, they found 1,393 animal skins—among them 581 leopard skins and 31 Bengali tiger skins. It was the single biggest haul since the People's Republic of China was founded in 1949, with a total street value in excess of US $1.2 million. Three Tibetans were arrested. The Indian handlers, organizers, and poachers managed to escape.

Like a drug addict reliant on animal parts for its everyday fix, China needs to be weaned off wildlife consumption if Asia's most endangered species are to have even a remote chance of survival. The process has already begun thanks to better education, the introduction of western medicine, and stricter enforcement. But it is not moving fast enough. Unless dramatic attitudinal changes take place across a broad spectrum of society, then the only rare wild animals left in Asia will be those seen in zoos.

"I don't think you can change the situation in five years and probably not even in ten," says Bill Jordan of the U.K.-based Bill Jordan Wildlife Defence Fund. "It's going to take at least a generation. And the question is what will be left by then?"

COUNTDOWN TO EXTINCTION

# THE IVORY TRAIL

In India, an ancient legend tells that many thousands of years ago elephants had the power to fly and that they roamed the clouds above the earth. But one day an unfortunate elephant landed on a banyan tree and fell through the roof of a hermit's hut underneath, destroying it. The angry hermit put a curse on the mighty beast, dooming it to remain on solid ground, deprived of flight forever.

Of all the world's animal species, none bears the symbolic importance for religions and nations equal to the elephant. Ganesh, the Hindu god of wisdom and knowledge, has the trunk and head of an elephant. The Buddha is sometimes represented as a snow white elephant. For centuries, entire nations would go to war over elephants. When the Siamese captured two auspicious white elephants in 1569, King Bayinnaung of Burma demanded that they be handed over immediately as gifts. When the Siamese refused, he attacked and ransacked their capital, Ayutthaya.

In many respects, the origins of the elephant are equally extraordinary. The largest of all living mammals, scientists trace its ancestry back some 50 million years. Its immediate predecessor is believed to have been a tapir-like creature with an extended snout. Further back in time, the elephant may even have been related to a type of whale known as the sea cow. From these beginnings, more than 300 elephant-like species evolved. They ranged from the woolly mammoth, with its tusks that extended more than two meters, to the dwarf-like pygmy elephant. But evolution has not been kind to the elephant. Today just two members of the species remain: the Asian elephant and the African elephant. And both of these are endangered.

During the 1970s and 1980s, gangs of poachers armed with automatic weapons rampaged through the forests and plains of Asia and Africa leaving a trail of bloated elephant corpses in their wake, their tusks crudely hacked out with machetes. Aided by powerful ivory syndicates and lobbyists around the world, "white gold" became a *de facto* underground currency that spawned a gigantic web of corruption and deceit. The figures were simply staggering. More than 2,000 African elephants were slaughtered every week to satisfy international demand. The raw ivory would be shipped to one of several laundering centers such as Dubai, the United Arab Emirates, or Hong Kong, before ending up on the "legal market." Eventually most of it would arrive in Japan, the biggest ivory market in the world.

The most shocking thing of all was that this charade was

Of the nearly three hundred varieties of elephant that once roamed the earth, only two remain—the Asian and the African elephants. Both are endangered.

OPPOSITE PAGE
**Hong Kong**
**November, 2003**
*Customs officers inspecting seized ivory.*

◁ For centuries, nations went to war over elephants, perceived to be representative of the beloved Hindu God Ganesh, giver of prosperity and good fortune, and remover of obstacles.

"A king who cares for the elephants like his own sons is always victorious, enjoying the friendship of the celestial world after death."

—*Kautiliya, Indian political thinker, 250 B.C.*

played out under the very eyes of CITES members whose task it was to oversee and regulate the international trade. Sustainable use of ivory became the popular mantra used to justify a limited commercial trade in ivory. The reality, however, was very different. This was a virtual free-for-all.

The bulk of the raw ivory was channeled through Hong Kong, the crown British colony whose very foundations had been built with the proceeds of the illegal opium trade. Between 1979 and 1989, Hong Kong imported more than 4,000 tons of ivory, equivalent to half a million dead elephants. In this freewheeling capitalist haven, the ivory was carved into exquisite jewelry, billiard balls, piano keys, and the meticulously sculpted personal stamps known in Japan as *hankos*. Owning an intricately carved ivory tusk became a status symbol throughout the region, akin to owning gold. Ivory pieces also found their way to Europe and North America, purchased as works of art or as an investment.

Despite growing international concern over the fate of the world's elephant population, numbers continued to decline, falling by 50 percent in less than a decade. By the mid-1980s, it looked like—barring a miracle—this animal could soon become extinct in the wild.

It took ten years for governments to wake up to the plight of the elephant. In 1988, the U.S. passed laws banning all imports of ivory. The following year, the parties to CITES agreed to place the elephant on the list of species facing possible extinction. The decision effectively granted the elephant the highest legal protection and prohibited any form of trade in ivory.

One third of an elephant's tusk is a pulp cavity full of blood and nerves embedded in the cranium. The visible tusk is composed of mostly dentine with an outer layer of enamel. This dentine is the ivory that we know so well. Viewing a cross section, one can see, with the naked eye, a diamond shaped pattern formed by a number of intersecting lines. This pattern is only found in elephant ivory and is why many purists say the only "true" ivory is elephant ivory.

By the mid-1990s, elephant populations in some African countries had already begun to recover as a result of strict enforcement in the U.S. and in other Western consumer markets. But in Asia, growing prosperity together with lax enforcement ensured that the illegal trade continued to flourish. In the fifteen years since the worldwide ivory ban was introduced, almost half of the region's elephant population has been wiped out. In countries like Vietnam, Laos, and Cambodia, the figure could be as high as 80 percent. Most of the ivory is turned into *objets d'art*, trinkets and souvenirs sold primarily in Thailand, Japan, and China, where the authorities have largely turned a blind eye.

To add to the woes of the Asian elephant, only males sport tusks. As a result, adult tuskers are specifically targeted by poachers. Today, in Kerala National Park in southern India, a spate of ivory-related killings has meant that there is just one mature male for every 122 mature females. The situation is now so critical that biologists like Vivek Menon, of the Wildlife Trust of India, warn that it could threaten the genetic makeup of the entire species.

The decimation of elephant populations in Asia is leading to a shift among criminal gangs that ply the trade. With ivory now fetching up to US $400 per kilo in China, profits are so high that African elephants are being killed to supply the burgeoning Asian market. The scale of the illegal trade was brought home in June 2002 when six tons of ivory—equivalent to 600 dead elephants—was discovered onboard a vessel transiting through the port of Singapore. The ivory originated in Zambia and had been shipped from Durban, South Africa, in wooden crates labeled as statues. Investigators believe that at least fourteen earlier shipments from Africa had successfully reached final destinations in Japan or China.

In a world where conservation is becoming increasingly linked to profit, the curse of the elephant is unlikely to go away. In 2002, the parties to CITES voted in principal to allow Botswana, Namibia, and South Africa to sell 60 tons of ivory from their existing stocks subject to a host of conditions. The bitterly fought decision could unleash a new bout of killing, since it is difficult and costly to tell the difference between African and Asian ivory.

Now some governments are openly calling for an end to the international ban on ivory trading on the grounds that populations have sufficiently recovered. If that happens, many conservationists fear that the largest and most powerful creature that walks the planet could yet find itself remembered only as the stuff of myths and legends. Three decades from now, the Asian elephant could quite literally cease to exist in the wild. "I cannot imagine a world without elephants," says Menon, one of the great authorities on the Asian elephant. "But can elephants withstand heightened levels of poaching for much longer?" 🐘

# DOES IT MATTER?

Hunter Weiler, a fast-talking American, who is a passionate wildlife conservationist and one-time big-game hunter, has a bizarre interest in an incongruous looking mammal. It has gigantic spiraled horns, a humped back, and the stature of an ox. It's also Cambodia's national animal.

King Sihanouk nominated the kouprey in 1964 when, as a young prince, he kept a kouprey calf in the palace gardens. A quarter of a century earlier, a kouprey was sent to Vincennes Zoo in Paris, where the previously unknown creature was studied by French scientists. Although it eventually starved to death during the German occupation, this was the first and only time that the kouprey has lived in captivity. Now, however, there is a problem: the kouprey has not been seen in the wilds of Cambodia for more than thirty years and many believe that it has joined the list of already extinct animals. "The kouprey is no more," says Weiler, who came to Cambodia in the late 1990s to search for the rare animal. "Based on everything I have seen and heard, I arrived just a little bit too late."

It is easy to dismiss the loss of the kouprey as insignificant in the greater scheme of things. After all, history is littered with extinctions ranging from the colossal Tyrannosaurus rex, which stalked the earth tens of millions of years ago, to the armor-plated, prehistoric lizard known as the sphenodontian. Barring the size and spectacular appearance of the dinosaurs, however, there is little to suggest that the world is any poorer for their absence.

Yet there is something profoundly different between the loss of prehistoric creatures and the rapid depletion of wildlife today. Previous extinctions were the work of nature: the earth's collision with a meteor, the advent of the Ice Age, or the evolution of a more sophisticated species. Far from being part of an evolutionary process, the recent loss of birds, mammals, and fish is almost wholly the work of man. And nothing on this scale has happened for millions of years.

Statistics only tell part of the story. But even in a world immune to natural disaster and driven forward by the single-minded pursuit of wealth, the numbers are too stark to ignore. Unless the current crisis is resolved, scientists from the United Nations Environment Program (UNEP) warn that up to a quarter of the world's mammals could vanish from the wild within the next thirty years. The list includes rhinos, tigers, Asian elephants, cheetahs, and mountain gorillas. In addition, one in eight bird species now faces a high risk of extinction, and at least 13 percent of the world's flowering plants could be about to perish. Some species are already so close to the brink that it would take almost nothing to push them over. There are fewer than 150 Chinese alligators surviving in the whole of China and there are less than 500 Philippine eagles in the Philippine archipelago.

If it were only a question of losing a few cuddly animals or areas of pristine forest, we could

*Kouprey, now believed to be extinct in Cambodia.*

△
Up to 42 percent of animal populations in Southeast Asia will be lost forever by the end of this century.
— World Wide Fund of Nature

put it down as a quirk of nature or the price of progress. But the issue goes far beyond conserving lions, tigers and elephants. The way that we treat wildlife is typical of the shortsighted way humans exploit every resource on the planet. Like a swarm of locusts, we devour everything in our path. Forests, fisheries, water, and farmland are consumed far quicker than nature can renew them. Widespread use of pesticides is poisoning the countryside. Yet in the face of this global rampage, the world's most powerful nations continue to squabble over the true nature of the threat. The crisis may not happen tomorrow, but happen it will—with devastating consequences. Even the naive conviction that technology and progress will allow us to defy the laws of nature cannot save mankind from the inevitable backlash.

The worst-case scenario is this. The first to go will be the big mammals that require the most land to survive and that help preserve vegetation and natural watersheds. When the big animals are gone, the subsequent effects will be felt throughout the animal and insect world. Slowly but surely the finely tuned natural order that has evolved over hundreds of millions of years will begin to falter. Vermin populations that are now kept in check will explode. Forests will become fragmented and die. The climate will change and the incidence of disease will rise. And ultimately, humanity, the most dominant animal of all, will find itself on an uninhabitable planet, a victim of its own hubris and unrelenting exploitation of natural resources.

If we allow this destruction to continue, what will happen when one day all the forests and wildlife are gone? Weiler has little doubt of the implications of this wholesale destruction. "It's like the canary in a coal mine," he says. "Each species extinction is a warning. If the warning is continuously ignored it is only a matter of time before a catastrophe happens."

More than simply a crime against nature, the killing of endangered species raises profoundly disturbing moral questions. What right do humans have to wipe out bird, plant, and mammal species that have taken millions of years to evolve? And why should we be able to pillage the earth now when our actions will deprive future generations of outstanding parts of their natural heritage? Our failure to save some of the world's best-known species could have other repercussions too. If we are unable to rescue the largest land mammals from the brink of extinction, what chance is there of protecting any lesser-known species? And what hope is there for saving ourselves?

On the island of Sumatra in Indonesia, there is a poignant reminder of what can happen when we interfere too much with the workings of nature. Formerly home to one of the biggest concentrations of orangutans on earth, only around 7,000 of these great apes still exist today. But rampant illegal logging and the loss of forests have done more than wipe out most of the orangutans. In late 2003, giant landslides tore down the mountainside, killing more than 100 villagers and tourists, uprooting trees, and leaving a trail of havoc in its wake. Only upturned houses, trees piled up like matchsticks, and collapsed roads and bridges remained—a stark reminder of humanity's powerlessness in the devastating face of nature.

Though many species appear to have trivial niches, we should remember that the relative effects of various organisms in biological systems are seldom static. Minor species can sometimes become very important as systems fluctuate.

*Kerry Bruce Clark*

# TIGER COUNTRY

Asitkumar Mondol doesn't remember much about the tiger that nearly killed him. The forty-two-year-old fisherman was out collecting crabs in the mangrove swamps of the Indian Sunderbans when he was attacked from behind. One of his companions was dragged screaming into the forest and never seen again. By the time Asitkumar was found, his skull had been ripped open like a ripe watermelon. It took eight hours to get him to the nearest hospital and he barely survived.

Heavily disfigured with a hole gauged out of the back of his scalp and a scar around his eye socket, Asitkumar is one of the lucky ones. Not far away from this remote corner of the Ganges Delta, there is a settlement known as the "village of widows." It is the place where more than 150 women have lost their husbands to the tigers of the Sunderbans. Despite fencing off large tracts of land and making offerings to Bonbibi, the supreme goddess and lady of the forest, the lack of prey species continues to turn tigers into man-eaters. And every year the number of widows continues to rise.

People like Asitkumar are simply trying to feed themselves and their families. Their only sin is to live on the edge of one of India's largest protected tiger reserves. If they don't go into the forest to collect honeycomb from the giant Himalayan bees or to search for crabs as their fathers have done before them, their families will have nothing to eat. But if they cross the narrow waterways into the mangrove forests and creeks, they risk being badly mauled or killed by one of nature's most dangerous predators. That is why black-and-white arguments about conservation do not always work. It's difficult to determine who is the hunter, who is the victim, and which side the law should be on.

The conflict between man and beast is an age-old one. But as roads and agricultural farming have ravaged the forests and as human populations have soared, the problem has reached critical levels. For tigers to survive in the wild, they require enormous tracts of forest, water, and mangrove. They also need prey species such as deer, sambar, and wild pig to feed on. Without the necessary food and habitat, these great wild animals, which some people are trying to preserve, turn into man-killers. In turn, poachers and villagers strike back with traps, spears, and guns, creating an endless cycle of death and destruction.

Tiger populations are in crisis throughout Asia. Hunting and habitat loss have imperiled

For tigers to survive in the wild, they require enormous tracts of forest, water, and mangrove. They also need prey species such as deer, sambar, and wild pig to feed on. Without the necessary food and habitat, these great wild animals, which some people are trying to preserve, turn into man-killers.

their future in the wild by fragmenting their populations and introducing the threat of inbreeding. Three of the eight species that roamed the jungles and forests at the beginning of the twentieth century are now extinct. Of the remaining five, two are listed as critically endangered. Nowadays, tigers are largely confined to small, isolated pockets of land, mainly in India, Bangladesh, and Nepal. With tiger skins and bones fetching thousands of dollars on the black markets in Asia, poachers are closing in on some of their last strongholds.

"We estimate the number of tigers at no more than 5,000 or 6,000," says Dr. Tony Lynam, at the Wildlife Conservation Society's office in Bangkok. Lynam and his colleagues have carried out extensive camera-trapping surveys of tiger populations in much of Asia. If their results are correct, it means more than 95 percent of the world's tiger population has been wiped out over the past 100 years.

The precipitous decline in the tiger population is all the more tragic given the immense respect with which it was once held. For centuries, forest-dwelling tribes in central India dared not mention the tiger's name directly but referred to it simply as the "Great One." In parts of Malaysia, some men were believed to have the ability to turn themselves into tigers. When the tiger was stripped of its mythical status by the arrival of missionaries and British, French, and Dutch colonials, the irrevocable decline began. Today, for millions of villagers, it is simply a pest or a source of undreamed of profit.

**Cambodia**
*Tiger trapped and shot in Cambodia.*

**Bankok, Thailand, 2003**
*Remains from large wildlife bust.*

If anybody should know about saving tigers, it is Dr. Ullas Karanth. One of a new generation of wildlife biologists with a background firmly grounded in science, Dr. Karanth has spent much of the past twenty years in India working for the Wildlife Conservation Society. Unlike many of his contemporaries, Karanth is far from downbeat about the outlook. "A century from now there could be 30,000 to 40,000 tigers in India alone," he says. "The real question is whether we can muster up the political will and raise the level of protection to make sure that this happens."

It's a radical vision and one that is far from the norm given that the demise of the tiger has been predicted for more than half a century. But Karanth, who earned a Masters Degree in wildlife at the University of Florida and recently wrote a book on tigers, believes that the conditions are already in place to support a far higher density of tigers. India alone has over 300,000 square kilometers of tiger habitat, but only about 10 percent of this is well protected. If that figure could be increased to 20 percent or 25 percent, it could create the conditions for a sharp rebound in tiger populations.

More than simply a stab in the dark, Karanth's predictions are firmly based on fact. Tigers have long proven their resilience in the wild and against all the odds have bounced back from the

**Raipur, Chatisgarh**
**India**
**1995**

*A tigress caught in a steel trap near Raipur. Tigers are often considered more valuable dead than alive in India as the poaching of these great creatures continues.*

△
There are five existing subspecies of tiger: Bengal, Indo-Chinese, Siberian, South China and Sumatran. Three sub-species of tiger became extinct in the last 70 years: Bali, Caspian and Javan.

> "As long as tigers and people continue to compete for space and sustenance, human-tiger conflicts will continue and aggravate the problems caused by commercial poaching."

brink of extinction on several occasions. With recent surveys identifying large amounts of potential tiger habitat in Thailand, Malaysia, Indonesia and parts of the Russian Far East, the hope now is that effective protection of key breeding populations could pave the way for a similar recovery.

Yet the same conditions that could ensure flourishing populations of tigers in Asia would also spell disaster for men like Asitkumar and the poor communities who must live alongside them. And while conservationists discuss ways of boosting the numbers of nature's greatest predators, locals in the Sunderbans are left wondering how big the "village of widows" will have to become before the world finally takes notice. 🦌

**Sunderbans**
**India**
**May, 2003**

*Asitkumar Mondol, age 42, was attacked by a tiger while foraging for crabs in the mangrove forests of the Sunderbans. While another of his companions was killed, Asitkumar survived horrendous head wounds and was dragged by a third companion for 8 hours before receiving medical attention. Here Asitkumar's wife attends to his wounds.*

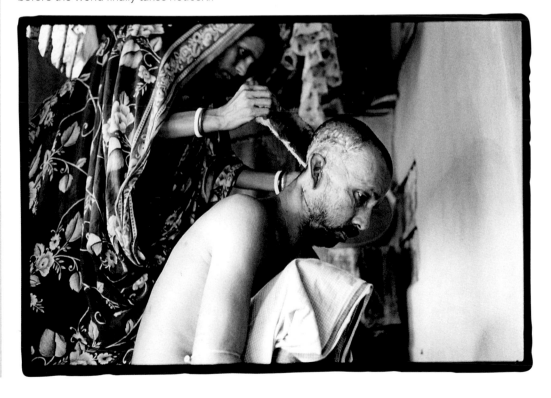

# FLEECING THE TIBETAN ANTELOPE

Gunji is a tiny settlement of around sixty inhabitants situated high in the mountains near the Indo-Tibetan border. It is an isolated trading post, only accessible during the summer months when the snow that blocks the surrounding passes has melted. Since the days of the British Empire, spices, *masalas*, and Tibetan medicines have been the main items available for barter here, painstakingly weighed out and exchanged for salt. However, for as long as anyone can remember, the people of Gunji have also traded in a fine type of wool known around the world as *shahtoosh*. These days it is spoken of in whispers.

In the spring of 1991, the internationally renowned biologist Dr. George Schaller was traveling through the cold, windswept plains of Tibet, far from Gunji, when he came across two dozen bloodied antelope carcasses stacked up outside a hunter's tent. Intrigued by the dead animals as well as by the sacks of wool traded in the nearby towns, Schaller inquired among the local people about the animals' origins. He also contacted conservationists around the region in order to discover what was behind the killings.

Over the next two years, the truth was slowly pieced together. High on the Tibetan plateau, extending from Lhasa to Ladakh in India, as many as 20,000 chiru, or Tibetan antelope, were being slaughtered for their fleece every year. The mass killings would take place in late-November and December in the winter rutting grounds or in May and June, when the females migrate to remote northern areas to bear calves. The antelope were easy prey for poachers. Armed with automatic weapons and using spotlights from four-wheel-drive vehicles to dazzle their victims, ruthless hunters would massacre the mothers in the darkness, leaving the newborn calves to be eaten by vultures.

Once the last adult chiru had been gunned down on the icy slopes, their valuable white down was plucked from their underbelly and throat. The fleece and the hide would then be carried for days over tortuous mountain passes before reaching the northern Indian states of Jammu and Kashmir. In this region, which is well known for having some of the finest weavers on earth, the exquisite under-fleece would be spun into wool known as *shahtoosh*, literally "the king of wool." The luxurious scarves and shawls would then be transported back over the border and sold openly as fashion items to the rich and famous not only in India, but as far away as London, Paris, and New York.

*Juvenile Tibetan antelope or Chiru.*

RIGHT
**Tibet**

*A herd of Tibetan Antelope migrate through the remote and inhospitable slopes of the Tibetan Plateau. These endangered creatures are massacred to produce fine shawls known as 'shahtoosh'.*

For centuries, *shahtoosh* has been prized above all other wool, thanks to its fine texture and exceptional lightness. Wealthy families from northern India would include it as part of their dowry. A *shahtoosh* shawl could be threaded through a wedding ring. One story tells how Napolean Bonaparte presented a shawl made of *shahtoosh* to his beloved Josephine. She was apparently so delighted that she ordered 400 more.

The bloody origins of the wool, however, had remained largely unknown—until recently. Among the most popular myths told to hide its origins was the Kashmiri traders' story that it came

To make one shawl, at least four antelope need to be killed. Over the past 100 years, as much as 90 percent of the chiru population has been slaughtered, leaving this gentle creature on the verge of extinction.

from wild mountain goats that molted tufts of hair during the summer, and that they simply gathered the molts from rocks and bushes. Some traders went so far as to say that the wool came from the extremely rare Siberian goose. The reality was somewhat different. To make one shawl, at least four antelope need to be killed. Over the past 100 years, as much as 90 percent of the chiru population has been slaughtered, leaving this gentle creature on the verge of extinction.

Schaller's findings set alarm bells ringing. While the chiru was already included on the list of animals protected under CITES, new enforcement measures were adopted by the international community. China established special anti-poaching forces to patrol the remote areas of Qinghai province, a mountainous region where hunting of chiru was rife. Representatives of the Indian government made a public commitment to clamp down on the illegal *shahtoosh* trade.

But while international and domestic laws have raised the level of protection for the Tibetan antelope, the killing of the chiru has not gone away. On these freezing barren plains, where during the winter months temperatures can fall to as low as -40ºC, many poor communities still depend on *shahtoosh* for their survival. To avoid detection, traders travel by bus, car, or yak, often stuffing sleeping bags or pillows with the rare wool to smuggle it over the Nepalese or Indian borders. Occasionally, dealers based in Tibet and China barter *shahtoosh* for tiger bones. The profits more than justify the risks. In Kashmir, a light-colored shawl without embroidery can sell for around US $500. By the time the finished shawls reach Europe or the U.S., they can sell for as much as US $18,000 apiece, netting huge gains for the middlemen.

△
The slaughter of tens of thousands of Tibetan Antelope, or chiru, annually for their wool has forced their populations to plummet to less than 75,000 animals from nearly one million at the beginning of the 20th century.
—TRAFFIC North America

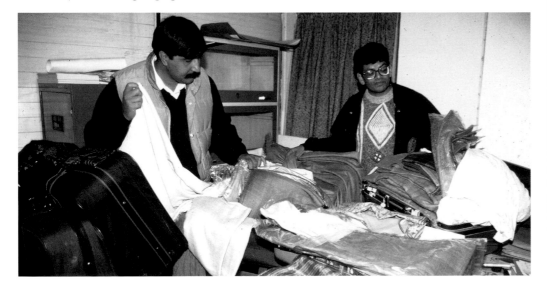

**Delhi, India, 1998**

*Under cover police in the Indian capital Delhi sort through a major seizure of shahtoosh shawls woven from the plucked hair of the endangered Tibetan Antelope. One shawl in Europe can sell for up to US $18,000 a piece.*

**Chang Tang, Tibet**

*Tibetan hunter with 22 chiru carcasses and several male heads (the hides are in the tent).*

Once in a long while, a major bust does take place. On April 7, 2003, Indian wildlife officials seized a consignment of 211 kilos of raw *shahtoosh* wool at a remote border crossing with Nepal. The haul equivalent to nearly 3,000 Tibetan antelopes was the biggest in the country's history. Three people were taken into custody. But the killers remained untouched. For Ashok Kumar, advisor to the Wildlife Trust of India and one of the first conservationists to establish the link between the trade in *shahtoosh* and the killing of the chiru, it was the final proof of the world's failure to stop the trade. "Despite all our efforts, Tibetan antelopes are still being killed. The wool of the chiru is still reaching India. There are as many shawls for sale this year in Delhi as last year. That is the reality."

There are some signs of hope that the world can save the chiru before it is too late. Confronted with new evidence over the terrifying fate of the Tibetan antelope, a number of the biggest icons in the fashion industry have pledged support against the use of *shahtoosh*. But as long as people remain ignorant of the plight of the chiru, this diminutive animal remains at risk. It would be a tragic irony if this creature, which endures some of the most inhospitable terrain on earth, were unable to survive human greed. 🐏

# SAVING THE RHINO

On a crystal clear morning in March, Chitwan National Park in southern Nepal echoed with the sound of gunfire. Less than fifty meters from a forest clearing, a great one-horned Asian rhino staggered and fell to the ground, where it lay virtually motionless until a group of men approached. The men worked quickly, checking the animal's abdomen and talking into two-way radios. The rhino was then hoisted into a wooden crate and driven off in a truck heading for the remote western border.

**Black Rhino**

△
Although only five species of rhinoceros precariously survive today, rhinos have a long and distinguished history. Since their origin about 50 million years ago, they have been an extremely diverse group, representing many different ecotypes and residing from temperate to arctic regions: some resembled giraffes, some horses, some hippos, while others were more like modern rhinos. Now extinct rhinos were once more widespread in North America and Europe than in Africa and Asia.

This sudden invasion in Nepal's best-known national park was not the work of poachers in search of the rhino's valuable horn, but an ambitious attempt by local and international conservationists to boost the rhino population by transporting small groups of the animals to new wildlife reserves. Named simply "Operation Rhino Translocation" it represents one of the biggest hopes that this animal, hunted for its valuable and densely matted horn, can be saved.

Of all the illegal forms of wildlife trade, the trafficking of rhino horn is the world's most secretive, profitable, and dangerous. Driven by the horn's extraordinary value (in some cases it's worth more than five times its weight in gold), it has long been the domain of powerful international syndicates. These ruthless operators attempt to control its supply and transport routes, much in the same way that oil and rubber barons attempted to corner their respective markets. Anyone who gets in the way is simply killed.

During the 1970s and 1980s, the war to control the lucrative rhino-horn market opened up a new front. In the face of soaring demand for rhino horn to make traditional Chinese medicine and ornamental dagger handles, a number of criminal syndicates banded together. The result was the formation of the world's most powerful rhino-horn cartel.

In early 1993, a team of undercover investigators from the U.K.-based Environmental Investigation Agency set out to expose the violent network of traffickers. Their first stop was to Africa, home of the biggest rhino population in the world. Steve Galster of WildAid in Bangkok was a member of the team. Galster, an American, has participated in countless undercover missions involving drugs, weapons, and wild animals. It was his responsibility to track the rhino horns to their ultimate destination. From the ports of Durban and Cape Town in South Africa, the trail led Galster thousands of miles over the Indian Ocean to a densely populated island off the coast of China. By

**Guwahati Zoo
India
May, 2003**

*A keeper at the Guwahati zoo touches one of the rhinos, while saying a small blessing.*

**Pabitora Wildlife Sanctuary
Assam, India
May, 2003**

*Rangers and police stand guard over a gang of Muslim poachers as they are questioned by the media. When the police searched the female member of the gang's house they found two rhino horns under her kitchen bench. The two horns were from a female rhino and her calf which had been poached two days earlier by means of electrocution.*

the early 1990s, Taiwan had become the world's center for rhino-horn smuggling. It had a stockpile estimated to total nine tons—equivalent to 3,700 dead rhinos—with a street value of US $50 million at the time. And the horns were openly on sale.

The trafficking routes, however, led beyond Taiwan to Guangzhou, a sprawling city of 6 million inhabitants in southern China. In the White Swan Hotel on the outskirts of town, Galster and his Taiwanese assistant Rebecca Chen, first made contact with men whose aim was to drive the rhino to extinction. "The smugglers believed that if the rhino became extinct, the price of rhino horn could easily have doubled," says Galster, who posed as a wealthy South African buyer of rhino horn. "This was a calculated attempt to corner the market using horns from one of the most valuable and endangered species on earth."

Galster learned that senior government officials were involved at every level of the operation. Diplomats from North Korea and South Korea were illegally importing the horn from South Africa to Taiwan in diplomatic pouches. Despite a blanket ban on all trade between the two countries, the consignments were then smuggled via Hong Kong to southern China. In the town of Zhiang

Jiang, near the border with Vietnam, semi-state officials stockpiled them in three warehouses. In one warehouse, Galster and Chen used concealed cameras to film 600 rhino horns poking out of potato sacks.

When Galster agreed to purchase 1.1 tons of rhino horn for cash, the Chinese sellers offered to arrange a military escort to accompany the shipment to the border with Hong Kong. From there the horn could have been sent anywhere in the world. Instead, Galster boarded a flight to Taiwan and then to London with the undercover film concealed on his body. The footage, together with other documentary evidence, was presented to a special CITES meeting held in Brussels. At least six officials involved in the illegal operation were rounded up and sent for trial.

Several months later, a surreal event occurred. As groups of eager Chinese onlookers watched spellbound, a mountain of rhino horn was burned in public, like a funeral pyre for all the world to see.

The unprecedented undercover operation, however, may well have saved the rhino from extinction. Following the introduction of new and tougher anti-trafficking measures, populations in some countries began to recover. As of 2002, there were close to 3,000 rhinos in Asia. Meanwhile in Africa, where some of the largest massacres had taken place, the numbers of black African rhino and white African rhino are also on the rise.

Even bigger news occurred in April 2000, when scientists from the World Wide Fund for Nature (WWF) using automatic infrared movement-triggered cameras were able to produce the first documentary evidence that the Javan rhino—the world's most endangered mammal—still existed in the wilds of Vietnam. The cameras confirmed what locals in the area had claimed for a number of years: that around seven to ten of these animals inhabited the Nam Cat Tien National Park in the country's southwest. The rediscovery of a species last seen in Vietnam in the early 1960s has set in motion frenzied efforts to pull this animal back from the brink of extinction.

Whether the rhino can survive in a world of depleted forests and fast-growing populations is likely to depend as much on continued international pressure from governments and conservationists as it is on preservation of their habitat. But there is a lesson that can be drawn from the battle to save the rhino: if the world is committed to stopping the trade in wildlife and it is prepared to use its full legal and financial muscle to do so, then it can and will be successful. ⅄

The world's few thousand black rhino are surviving in about 60 scattered populations, most of these living in relatively small conservation areas, and the total population is still falling due to poaching. The poachers, unwittingly or not, are directly contributing to the extinction of this magnificent animal.

**Chitwan National Park**
**Bharatpur, Nepal**
**January, 2004**

*At the Bharatpur barracks, a Royal Forestry Department Officer holds a rhino poached for its horn. The stockpile of items is five years old and the value is an estimated US $750,000.*

# THE WHALE SHARKS OF VERAVAL

On the west coast of India, where the state of Gujarat juts out into the Arabian Sea, the start of the monsoon rains brings a familiar pattern. Whale sharks, with white spotted fins and heads the size of battering rams, congregate in these dazzling tropical waters attracted by countless millions of plankton and other microscopic organisms. The arrival of these gigantic creatures, some of which measure up to fourteen meters in length, has long been a signal for the people of Veraval, one of India's major fishing ports, to take to their boats. Climbing into small rickety vessels, they would risk their lives trawling the great oceans in search of the whale shark, which is the world's largest fish and possibly its oldest. The shark is believed to migrate to the shores of India from as far away as Australia.

Until recently, the beginning of the monsoon also heralded the start of a killing spree so savage that the shallow waters of Veraval turned red with blood. Every year up to a thousand whale sharks were killed for their meat, fins, liver, and cartilage. When a whale shark was sighted far out to sea, the fishermen would sail close enough to fire an 8- to 10-kilogram harpoon into its shoulder or gills. Then they would insert a second hook tied to a barrel into the fish's pectoral fin. The normally docile fish would become agitated, diving or swimming away from the boat in a futile bid to escape.

Sometimes, the battle lasted six or seven hours before the whale shark finally exhausted itself. Once the creature had been brought to the surface, it would be towed to land and butchered with knives and spears, often while still alive. Its liver was cut into strips and placed in metal drums that were left out in the sun. Over time, the liver turned into an oil that was used to waterproof fishing boats or to manufacture shoe polish. A liter of the oil fetched less than US $1, a tiny amount by Western standards but a godsend to the people of Veraval. Meat from the shark was occasionally frozen and exported to Taiwan.

In 1996, Indian wildlife-filmmaker Mike Pandey began work on a documentary about the slaughter and trade of the whale shark, which is known locally as the *badi machli*. Driven by memories of his childhood, when he saw these magnificent creatures diving playfully alongside

**Veraval, Gujarat**
**India**

*These photos are of a whale shark on the coast of Gujarat, a major maritime state in India with the longest coastline (1,640 km) and widest continental shelf (36 per cent of India's continental shelf area). According to a trade report conducted by TRAFFIC India in 2001 on the coast of Gujarat, each whale shark sells between Rs 40,000 to Rs 1,50,000 (US $900-3400). Its fins, meat, liver, cartilage, skin, viscera and teeth are sold separately. The separation of parts and removal of liver and other body parts is done at Veraval while its neighboring townships like Okha and Dhamlej, are involved in their dispatch to market.*

the passenger ship that first brought his family to India, he inquired among government officials, marine biologists, and fishermen as to its whereabouts. He was told that the whale shark had never existed in Indian waters.

It took almost three years for Pandey and his film crew to track down these mysterious creatures along the shores of Gujarat and to film them being dragged ashore and mercilessly butchered by the local fishermen. The film finally brought to the attention of the world the fate of this rapidly dwindling species. In May 2001, Pandey's efforts paid off, when India granted the whale shark endangered species status and banned all commercial fishing of the animal. Eighteen months later, CITES awarded it protected status.

For Pandey, an environmentalist who has spent a lifetime working on films about man's conflict with the elephant and other species that inhabit this earth, *The Silent Shores* represented one of his career's greatest achievements. Its heartfelt message also brought home the fragile bond between man and nature that is fast disappearing in the face of greed and progress. "If you want to bring real change to this world, you have to touch the hearts and open the eyes of the people—not the governments," he said from his small studio in Delhi, where he is now working on a film about tigers. "We are custodians of this earth. Yet we have become the destroyers."

Tall, eloquent, and passionate about what he does, Pandey is in many respects a lone voice in the wilderness. But it is people like him who are making a difference by demanding that we stop to think about our own lives and the impact we are having on species that existed millions of years before we arrived on this earth.

If the whale sharks of Gujarat are no longer under direct threat, unregulated, commercial shark fishing continues to leave a bloody trail through Asian waters. Every day, Hong Kong, the center of the world's shark fin trade, imports over 16 metric tons of dried shark fin, shipped from as far away as Yemen, South Africa, and Kenya. It is then re-exported to mainland China, Taiwan, and Singapore.

The fins are mainly used for shark fin soup, a 2,000-year-old Chinese delicacy believed to improve a person's *feng shui*, boost women's vitality, and demonstrate a man's prosperity. Legends tell that in ancient times, a family's entire reputation depended on the quality of their shark fin soup. On occasions, unfortunate chefs were beheaded when their broth failed to live up to expectations. Like many traditions, the practice of serving up shark fin soup has continued to this day despite the fact that the fin has no taste. In plush restaurants scattered around Hong Kong, shark fin soup can sell for up to US $100 a bowl. So intertwined is it with Chinese culture, that a wedding ceremony or New Year's banquet is considered incomplete without copious servings of the stuff.

Behind the colorful legends that surround this exquisitely served dish is a multimillion dollar industry that operates with utter brutality. To avoid bringing the sharks ashore, a time-consuming and costly exercise, fishermen simply cut off the fins with bloodied machetes. The writhing creatures are then flung back into the waters where they are either eaten by other sharks or die a slow and agonizing death by suffocation. Such is the lobbying power and profits of these giant industrial enterprises that efforts to regulate the trade in Asia have largely floundered in a sea of lies and deception. When WildAid launched a high-profile campaign against the consumption of shark fin soup in Thailand, they were slapped with a US $3-million lawsuit by restaurateurs who claimed the ads were misleading and had adversely affected their business.

Besides the needless cruelty, the mass slaughter of sharks raises another frightening possibility. In the past half century, the shark population has plunged in some species by over 80 percent. The disappearance of sharks is in turn leading to declines of other marine species. "Sharks are the top predators in the world's oceans," says Victor Wu of WildAid, one of the leading international campaigners fighting the trade. "Despite their unpopular appearance, they have a crucial role in maintaining the balance and health of marine ecosystems."

Fortunately, a medley of high-profile figures has added their voices to the chorus of environmentalists attempting to wean Asians from shark fin soup. In late 2001, the daughter of Taiwanese president Chen Sui-bian was married in a traditional ceremony in Taipei. The wedding was touted as *the* high-society wedding of the year, and it was attended by some of the country's most distinguished Chinese families. In an important departure from tradition, the menu included oyster soup instead of the traditional shark fin delicacy. The replacement was made explicitly on environmental grounds. ₰

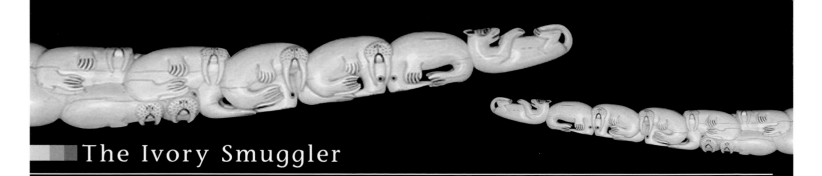

# The Ivory Smuggler

It was the eyes that gave Mohammed Sanoussy away—his eyes, together with the fact that the man attempting to pass through a line reserved for airline crew and diplomats was neither an embassy official nor a member of any airline. That mistake cost Sanoussy the chance to obtain a hefty cut of the US $25,000 the ivory in his bag was worth. It also led to the Thai authorities arresting him.

Sanoussy had come from Oman, one of many bounty hunters looking to make a killing. He had taken the twice-weekly Gulf Air flight from Muscat that arrives at Bangkok International Airport at about 10:15 a.m. When customs officials stopped him, they discovered sixty large pieces of ivory weighing 195 kilograms—the equivalent of nineteen dead elephants.

The day after Sanoussy arrived in Thailand, another shipment of ivory was found in four pieces of unclaimed luggage at the airport. The ivory had been transported on the same Gulf Air flight from Muscat, suggesting that it was due to be collected by the same man. Sanoussy was taken into police custody where he was charged with bringing smuggled goods into Thailand and with violating the National Wildlife Conservation Act. Several days later, he signed over the ivory to the government and was released.

To find one of the major ivory carving centers in Thailand, you must drive three hours north of the capital to the town of Phayuha Kiri. For at least a generation, this prosperous little town has been the ivory capital of Thailand. One ivory shop is said to have been there for almost 200 years. Like many traditional skills in the country, ivory carving is on the wane. But as recently as 2001, Phayuha Kiri still boasted fifty craftsmen mainly working freelance out of their own homes.

Inquisitive foreigners, however, are not welcome. Within minutes of our arrival, locals were alert to the presence of potential troublemakers. A brand new Isuzu four-wheel drive cruised slowly alongside us as we walked down the street and a driver checked us out carefully. It's only a warning, but in Thailand, as numerous incidents have proved, warnings such as this are to be taken seriously.

The craftsmen of Phayuha Kiri have good reason to be on their guard. In March 2001, private investigators counted 39,649 individual items made from ivory displayed in twelve shops along the main road. Most of the ivory is wholesale, destined for tourist shops in Bangkok where it is sold at prices marked up five- to six- times.

The Thai authorities claim that ivory comes from domesticated elephants, which are not subject to the international ban. But the reality is different. In late 2002, Thailand was named by CITES as one of the world's major ivory trafficking centers. Since then, several more illegal ivory hauls have been seized at Bangkok International Airport including sixty-five elephant tusks worth US $70,000. The consignment, which was labeled as gems, had arrived on a flight from Ethiopia. Given the high demand for ivory in Thailand, it is unlikely to be the last.

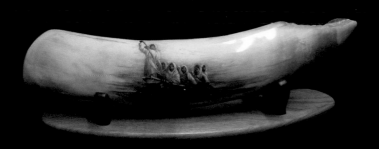

△ A piece of ivory like this one can sell for up to US $15,000. As the stockpiles of ivory are being sold off, so the demand for more ivory increases. This demand is met by illegal poaching which continues at high levels.

# THE LAST OF THE ORANGUTANS

From a lush hillside on the Indonesian island of Sumatra, Dr Ian Singleton, a 39-year-old scientist from Hull is directing efforts to save the Sumatran orangutan. For a man who has spent the greater part of his adult life studying primates, it's an immensely rewarding task. In a nearby enclosure, two orangutans formerly kept as pets, play together, unaware that they will shortly be released back into the wild as part of an ongoing rehabilitation program. Dr. Singleton acknowledges, however, that unless more is done to halt the destruction of the forests and the activities of poachers his efforts will be in vain. "Without urgent action, the Sumatran orangutan will be the first of the great apes to become extinct," he says.

The word 'orangutan' in the Malay language literally translates as 'person of the forest.' Scientific research has revealed that man shares 96% of his genetic make-up with the orangutan. Ironically, this primate's large brown eyes and human-like behaviour have made it a popular trophy pet amongst rich Asians. Of the hundreds of thousands that existed at the beginning of the last century, the number of Sumatran orangutans has fallen to an estimated 7,000 in the wild today. Most of them live in scattered populations in the fast shrinking forests of Indonesia.

There they make easy pickings for the local villagers who hunt them down, often hired by wealthy traders, big businessmen or the military which is heavily involved in illegal logging. Precise figures are hard to come by. But what is known is this. Before a baby orangutan can be captured, the mother will almost inevitably be shot. Frequently the traumatized offspring also die after falling from trees or as a result of the shocking conditions in which they are subsequently kept. For every baby orangutan illegally sold to a private collector, at least three others will die along the way.

From Indonesia many of the orangutans are smuggled by boat to Thailand. Edwin Wiek is a Dutchman who understands the darker side of the trade. He runs the acclaimed Wildlife Friends of Thailand rescue centre, situated 160 km south of Bangkok. The sanctuary has taken in more that its fair share of langurs as well as gibbons, bears and macaques. Some of them had been kept as pets; others arrived at the centre high on methamphetamines after being forced to work long hours performing in shows for tourists. In the most serious case of wildlife trafficking that he has ever come across, Wiek is currently investigating how as many as 100 orangutans were smuggled out of Indonesia to a private zoo in Thailand named Safari World. For years, Safari World ran orangutan boxing matches. "This could be the world's biggest case of ape smuggling," says Wiek, who has been lobbying for the animals to be sent back to Indonesia and released in the wild. "All we want is for justice to be served."

Despite his own formidable efforts and the support of various international conservation groups, Wiek has faced opposition at almost every step of the way. A year after the police first uncovered large numbers of unregistered orangutans at Safari World, the normal procedures for confiscating animals held illegally have yet to be fully implemented. Moves to carry out DNA tests in order to prove without any doubt that the primates come from Indonesia have also encountered a string of unforeseen difficulties. Meanwhile, Wiek has discovered that orangutans are being held illegally in other zoos and private collections both in Thailand and in neighbouring Cambodia.

That's bad news for Dr Singleton and the many biologists who have identified the organgutan as a keystone species that must be preserved at any cost. "Orangutans play a vital role in maintaining the rain forest eco system, particularly as dispersers of seed," says Dr. Singleton. "Their survival is critical to our understanding of great apes in Asia and ultimately to our understanding of the origins of the human race itself."

# FORGOTTEN SPECIES

**Every three or four years, the International Union for Conservation of Nature and Natural Resources (known as the IUCN) produces a document called the *Red List of Endangered Species*. Recognized as the world's most comprehensive data on the status of endangered species, it lists not only all the plants and animals in danger of extinction, but also those under threat.**

Even if you have precious little interest in the fate of the world's wildlife, you are bound to recognize a handful of the 11,000-odd species. There's the giant panda, beloved by Chinese emperors, who kept them in their palace gardens. There's the Malayan sun bear, whose last forest strongholds are under assault in the wilds of Malaysia, Thailand, and Vietnam. And there's the diminutive Irrawaddy dolphin, a creature found more commonly in aquariums than in the great rivers of Cambodia and Laos.

Turn the pages listing the rare and beautiful creatures which may one day be erased forever and you will also come across the names of thousands of other birds, mammals, reptiles, and fish. These are the forgotten species, many of whom may soon be found only in zoos or illegal private collections.

High up on the shopping list of collectors of exotic wildlife is the Komodo dragon. First discovered by a Dutch scientist in 1912, this gigantic lizard is now so rare that there are probably fewer than 5,000 of them left in the wild. Dealers with the right contacts, however, can still buy one on the black market for around US $30,000. It's a similar story with the Chinese alligator known as *Tu Long*, or the "earth dragon." At last count this much sought-after reptile numbered fewer than 150 outside of captivity, mainly in the lower Yangtze River valley in China. But so popular is the Chinese alligator that people are prepared to pay up to US $8,000 for one on the black market.

Why would anyone want to own a Komodo dragon, which can bite a man's leg off, or a Chinese alligator? The reason is pathetically simple. Collecting rare and illegal wildlife is a matter of immense prestige for the rich and powerful. And the more difficult a wild animal is to obtain, the greater the status it confers on its owner, who demonstrates that he or she is above the law.

That's why people like Lawrence Wee Soon Chye, a thirty-eight-year-old Singaporean, first became involved in the trade. Chye was eventually caught smuggling large numbers of Indian star tortoises and monitor lizards into the U.S. in boxes labeled as books, magazines, and lamps. He's

> Collecting rare and illegal wildlife is a matter of immense prestige for the rich and powerful.

now in jail in Florida, sentenced to thirty-seven months' imprisonment for the illegal trafficking of endangered species.

There are even stranger fetishes, however than owning an Indian star tortoise, a foul-smelling lizard, or a highly poisonous snake. In Japan, stag beetles such as the lustrous green yanbaru are in such demand as pets that in August 1999 a nearly 8-cm-long male stag beetle was sold to a private collector for a record US $92,240. Now the search is on for bigger and even more striking specimens, leading to rampant poaching in neighboring countries. In the remote Yumsom forest in Sikkim, several Japanese nationals have been arrested with sacks full of the *chimte kira*, an indigenous stag beetle found in the foothills of the Himalayas. Collected during the rainy season from June to September, they sell locally for as little as US $10. By the time they reach Japan, the price will have risen at least twenty-fold.

These days even scorpions and spiders are in big demand around the globe. "People have less time and less space," says Dr. Barbara Maas, head of Care for the Wild International. "They want something that is exotic and a little crazy and which fits on the shelf."

Dr. Maas, a recognized authority on the capture and transportation of wild animals, has long campaigned to raise awareness about the severe physical trauma, stress and disease sustained during export. The statistics are shocking. Mortality rates of up to 50% have been reported for wild-caught primates imported into the US. In the case of ornamental fish, the figure is as high as 80%.

But in this twilight world where stag beetles can sell for more than a Rolls Royce, all is not lost. In 1992, John Mackinnon, a biologist working for the World Wide Fund for Nature (WWF), was surveying a nature reserve in northern Vietnam when he sighted a large ox that resembled an African oryx antelope. The chestnut-and-black ox since named the saola was only the fourth large land mammal to be discovered in the twentieth century. Two years later, the world's smallest species of muntjac deer was also identified in the Annamite Mountain Range, which straddles the Lao–Vietnam border.

Far from giving up on the idea of identifying new species or rediscovering endangered ones, scientists working in remote areas of Burma and the Cardamom Mountains of Cambodia believe there could be plenty of other unknown creatures living in the last wildernesses of Asia. In 1812, the French naturalist Georges Cuvier wrote that "there is little hope of discovering new species of large quadrupeds," notes George Schaller, one of the world's most respected conservationists. "The saola and others proved his prediction wrong. There is every reason to believe that the forest's shadows may still shroud other mysterious creatures."

# FIVE

## THE BATTLE FOR CONSERVATION

# THE RUSSIAN FAR EAST

The city of Vladivostok is situated less than 100 kilometers from the border with China in the vast snow-covered wilderness known as the Russian Far East. Closed off to all non-Soviets until 1991 because of its strategic position as home base of the Russian Pacific fleet, it is today a thriving entrepot for trade with Asia. Countless shipping offices, brothels, hotels, and banks crowd around this maritime city, which still plays host to Russia's busiest commercial fishing fleet. But like so much of this crime-ridden country, many of these operations have direct links to organized Russian and Chinese gangs, whose interests extend from the trafficking of women and drugs to arms and animal parts.

Shortly after midnight on 2 April 2000, armed officers from the Russian Police Force backed up by the Federal Security Service swooped down on a hotel parking lot in Vladivostok. Hidden inside a white Toyota Corolla, they discovered skins of the rare Siberian tiger. A high-ranking police officer suspected of being at the heart of one of the nation's biggest smuggling operations was immediately apprehended. Within seventy-two hours of the sting, enforcement agents moved in to arrest two more groups of wildlife dealers linked to Chinese criminal gangs from over the border.

It was the climax of an operation that had begun several years earlier in a last-ditch attempt to save the Siberian tiger from almost certain extinction. For more than half a century, Soviet authorities had protected Russia's extraordinarily rich and diverse wildlife. But when the Iron Curtain came down, so did Soviet protection for the country's wild animals. In the free-for-all that followed, poaching gangs hunted down everything of value using helicopters, snowmobiles, and land cruisers, transforming the Russian Far East into a gigantic killing ground. In just three years, half of its musk deer population had been wiped out. By the mid-1990s, only around 200 Siberian tigers were left in the wild. Those animals that survived were mercilessly hunted down for profit.

The first major breakthrough in the desperate battle to save the Siberian tiger came when agents from Russia's Inspection Tiger, a specialized wildlife protection unit, successfully infiltrated one of the most notorious Russian-Chinese organized crime rings. The investigation team learned that Siberian tigers, Amur leopards, and Himalayan bears were being killed in the remote forests

*Siberian Tiger*

**Primorsky Krai Russia**

*"Operation Amba" (Department Tiger) officials burning Siberian tiger skins confiscated from poachers in Primorsky Krai, Russian Far East.*

that blanket the sparsely populated Far East region, then taken by road to the border checkpoint at Poltovka. From here they were smuggled into northeast China.

In March 2000, the net began to close. Acting on a tip-off, Russian customs officers seized a truck full of animal skins, bear paws, and other wildlife parts heading for the Chinese border. The sting provided investigators with the last crucial piece of evidence that they needed to move against the powerful criminal syndicate. After three years of painstaking work, the final stage of the operation could begin.

At around 7:00 p.m. on a cool April evening, Sergei Bereznuk, a tough no-nonsense Russian who had spent much of the past decade fighting wildlife traffickers, telephoned Andrey Korolev, a police officer believed to be at the center of the illegal operation. Bereznuk claimed he was in the company of a wealthy foreigner interested in buying large numbers of tiger skins. "I told him that I had got his name from a mutual contact," said Bereznuk, who now works for Phoenix Fund, a local conservation organization.

Convinced that Bereznuk and his colleague Steve Galster were bona fide dealers, police officer Korolev instructed the two men to drive to the city of Ussurisk, 100 kilometers north of Vladivostok, and to wait outside the post office in the center of town. At around midnight, a white Toyota pulled up in front of the building and the two men were instructed to follow. Wearing hidden cameras and trailed by armed police, Bereznuk and Galster were taken to an empty apartment block. There they negotiated to buy two Siberian tiger skins as part of a larger consignment. "I held up the skins so that Steve could clearly film them using a secret camera," recalled Sergei, who was pretending to be the middleman.

Once the deal had been sealed, the investigators asked Korolev to deliver the tiger skins to a hotel parking lot in Vladivostok, where they promised to hand over the money. It took little more than an hour to reach the parking lot. Undercover enforcement agents were waiting. At around 2:30 a.m. they ambushed the corrupt police officer and took him into temporary custody on charges of illegal wildlife smuggling.

The sting, followed hours later by a second and then a third seizure, sent shock waves through the underground networks in Russia and China. Within a period of just thirty-six hours, an entire poaching network trading wildlife worth at least US $5 million a year had been brought to its knees. But in a country where criminal gangs still operate with virtual impunity and where more than a dozen wildlife enforcement officers have been gunned down in the past decade, the battle is far from over.

Hundreds of kilometers north of Vladivostok in the remote Sikhote-Alin Mountains, a group of Russian and American biologists is also trying to save the Siberian tiger. The researchers, who are part of the Siberian Tiger Project, rely on a technique called radiotelemetry to tranquilize tigers, fit them with special radio transmitter collars, then release them back into the wild. The collars send radio signals that enable team members like John Goodrich to track the animals' movements as they range through the temperate forests in search of prey.

The Siberian Tiger Project is the brainchild of Maurice Hornocker and Howard Quigley of the Hornocker Wildlife Institute, which is now part of the Wildlife Conservation Society. Acclaimed as the longest-running project of its kind, it seeks to find out everything there is to know about this tiger subspecies in order to ensure its survival.

Since the first tiger—a one-year-old cub named Olga—was radio-collared back in February 1992, the team has caught and collared another thirty-seven wild tigers, nine of which are still sending out signals. Their painstaking research has brought to light some stunning discoveries. Each female tiger requires an average of 450 square kilometers to successfully rear cubs in the wild. Young tigers, in turn, may wander up to 240 kilometers in search of their own territory. A more disturbing finding by Goodrich and his colleagues is that humans cause more than 80 percent of all tiger deaths in Russia.

The revelation has only served to highlight the importance of the project. "The goal is to collect the best ecological data possible for use in conservation planning," says Goodrich, who acts as the principal field coordinator. "By capturing and outfitting tigers with radio collars, we have been able to study tiger social structure, land-use patterns, food habits, reproduction, and mortality patterns and the tiger's relations to other inhabitants of the ecosystem."

It is a mission that is fraught with challenges and uncertainties. Nonetheless, it has thrown a lifeline to one of the rarest creatures on the planet. Latest estimates put the number of adult Siberian tigers in the wild at between 330 and 370. The figure is still critically small, but it's a lot larger than it was a decade ago. Some Siberian tigers are even moving into areas where they have not been seen in years. Conservationists hope that this information will provide the sort of inspiration necessary to gain further public support for groundbreaking scientific programs. "I think there is perhaps more hope for Amur (Siberian) tigers than any other species, because there is a very large, intact piece of habitat with very low human densities," says Goodrich. " I suppose that's the lesson. Protect the habitat, and the fewer people, the better." 🦌

Organized criminal gangs including the Russian Mafia and drugs cartels are trading in highly profitable wildlife products by using existing smuggling routes for illegal commodities, such as small arms, drugs and humans.

**Far East, Russia
Early 1990s**

*After stripping the skins, bear poachers load them into helicopters for transport.*

# A POACHER'S TALE

Prawing Klinkai claims to have killed at least seventy elephants in his lifetime. That represents roughly 140 ivory tusks, 70 elephant tails, and 280 elephant legs. Sold on the black market they would have a combined street value in excess of US $300,000 in the West. But all the weather-beaten poacher from northeast Thailand earned was about US $15,000 over a period of ten years, barely enough to support his six brothers and sisters.

Born into a small rice-farming village a few hours drive from Bangkok, Prawing remembers from his very earliest days going out into the forests of the Dongrak mountain range with his family to hunt for wild animals. Sometimes they would kill wild boar or pig, and on other occasions deer or hog badgers. The meat would help supplement the family's meager diet of rice and vegetables, which was all that a poor household in this district could afford.

At the age of eighteen or nineteen Prawing swapped his old flintlock rifle for an AK-47. The automatic weapon, a birthday present from his father, was capable of killing almost any type of wild animal. It was not long before Prawing began to use it to full effect. "The first time that I killed an elephant was at the request of a local official, who promised to pay me about US $150 per kilo for the ivory tusks," he says. Hoping to make extra money, Prawing also hacked off the elephant's ears and penis, which he offered for sale. But the local buyer cheated him, paying only half the price originally agreed.

That setback didn't deter Prawing for long. Soon the small-time rice farmer started hunting for money on a regular basis. Mostly, he supplied ivory to local traders, who sold it to big dealers at a hefty markup. At one stage, Prawing was even approached by a government or military official—who he can't name—to kill elephants down in Malaysia. "I never felt bad about killing elephants at the time because the law was not enforced and all I cared about was looking after my family," he says.

Now aged forty-one, Prawing still looks apprehensive when asked too many questions. His refusal to name the people he was involved with at that time is understandable. In February 1998, Boomee Dairerk, a wizened old villager from Thailand's northeast was gunned down after

**Kaeng Krachan
Thailand
October, 2003**

*Former ivory poacher Prawing Klinkai has become a tracker and conservationist employed by The Wildlife Conservation Society.*

# "It will take time to stop the hunting. When people are poor and hungry they will try to make money in whatever way they can." — Former Elephant Poacher Prawing Klinkai

he went public about the lucrative ivory trade in Khao Yai, one of Thailand's biggest national parks. Boomee was a former fragrant-wood forager who knew all about the illegal activities in the area and had become the eyes and ears for conservationists. The old man was not the only activist to pay for his newfound beliefs with his life. Two years earlier, Uncle Jan, another elderly villager was cut down in a hail of bullets because he knew too much about the involvement of local godfathers and influential businessmen.

Prawing was such a successful hunter that he also received death threats. His name was mentioned in the local newspaper alongside other well-known poachers. Prawing and his family became frightened. Looking for a way out, the wiry-framed poacher eventually gave up hunting and went back to rice farming.

These days, Prawing works in a very different capacity. Recruited by an international conservation group, he still spends much of his time combing Thailand's forests looking for animal tracks. But this time it's as a guide, working with a team of armed national park rangers.

Occasionally Prawing visits schools and communities to help teach villagers about the importance of the forests and wildlife, and to encourage them to seek alternative sources of employment. He prefers not to get directly involved with poachers, however, because he fears they will bring up his past.

Down the road from Khao Yai, in the village of Ban Non Saen Suk, another experiment that is underway could have even bigger repercussions for the future of conservation. Once a hotbed of poachers and illegal aloe-wood collectors, the inhabitants of this poor hamlet have been persuaded to trade their weapons and snares for funds to grow organic vegetables. They now produce shiitake

*Elephants play a crucial role in patrolling protected areas and accessing wilderness areas. Unfortunately they also contribute to their own downfall when used by humans for logging operations and clearing forest.*

mushrooms as well as edible crickets and chickens, which are sold in the local markets. It's not big money. But it's enough to support the families and ensure they won't be forced to go hunting in the forests again because of economic hardship.

The Khao Yai Conservation Program has proved so effective it could eventually become a model for conservation programs throughout Asia. If that happens, it will not be a moment too soon. Protecting wildlife is an immensely complex issue and to see it purely in terms of enforcement or community-based programs is to miss out on the bigger picture. Like the war on drugs or the battle against human traffickers, the key to conservation is to work on a multitude of different, but integrated fronts. And programs like Khao Yai may be just the answer.

When asked if it is possible to halt the illegal trade once and for all, Prawing is silent for a moment before answering. "It will take time to stop the hunting," he says. "When people are poor and hungry they will try to make money in whatever way they can. But now the children are growing up with a new awareness of conservation and a better education than when I was young."

In many ways, Prawing's situation is little different from a host of other poor villagers. For years, he took the biggest risks and was paid the smallest share of the profits. Throughout Asia, there are tens of thousands of people like Prawing who will turn to hunting if times get tough. Until they are given another means of employment or an alternative way of making a profit, efforts to stop the trade are doomed to failure. "You can do all the raids you like. But if people don't have an alternative, they will go back to hunting time and time again," says Brian Kennerley, a wildlife enforcement advisor from New Zealand who spent several years working in Asia.

And that's the brutal reality. Blame it on poverty. Blame it on corruption or greed. But ultimately if the wealthy nations of the world are not prepared to offer anything in return, why should these farmers give up hunting, an activity that they have practiced for generations, simply so that we can enjoy the luxury of viewing pristine nature? ✍

# WILDLIFE RESCUE

The Phnom Tamao Wildlife Rescue Center sits on a 70-hectare site, a short distance south of the Cambodian capital Phnom Penh. Its leafy enclosures play host to tigers, bears, pileated gibbons, and even the rare sarus crane, of which there are less than 1,000 left in the world. Its cages are large and open. But Phnom Tamao has another unique claim to fame. Almost all of the animals kept here have been confiscated from poachers or illegal traders. And with the exception of creatures caught in traps or kept too long in human captivity, they will eventually be released back into the wild.

Supported by a bevy of international names and a team of animal husbandry and veterinary experts, Phnom Tamao is the most visible sign of Cambodia's halting attempts to clean up the illegal wildlife trade under the watchful eye of international donors. As an added bonus, it also plays a vital role in educating local people about the problems of the trade and the importance of preserving the country's wildlife and habitat. If all goes according to plan, the rescue center may even bring in much needed tourist revenues for the country's cash-strapped government. Nick Marx is one of two expatriates who works at Phnom Tamao, caring for the animals that are brought in, some of them in the most miserable condition. "Every animal in Phnom Tamao has a story," he says. "One day it could be a macaque or a civet that is brought here after being rescued from a trader. The next, it could be 100 storks."

One of the best stories that Nick tells is of Oral, the three-legged Malaysian sun bear who was destined to be eaten in one of the local restaurants but was saved and taken to the rescue center. Oral is now recovering in a spacious cage filled with branches and leaves. Then there's the serow that arrived half dead from bites to his head, neck, and body. The goat-like creature survived after receiving round-the-clock care from staff at the center.

The biggest story of all, though, is the reason so many animals found their way here in the first place. Back in early 2000, a wealthy American heiress by the name of Suwanna Gauntlett swept into town with grand plans to stop the illegal wildlife trade once and for all. Gauntlett witnessed bear paws being eaten in the restaurants of Phnom Penh and saw rare animals openly traded on the roadsides and in the markets. She vowed to take action. Aware that the government had neither the funds nor the willpower to tackle the problem head on, Gauntlett took matters into her own hands. The

**Bokor National Park
Cambodia
January, 2003**

*A disorientated Slow-Loris that has been rescued by members of the Cambodian National Forestry Department is set free.*

result is the Wilderness Protection Mobile Unit, Cambodia's equivalent of a SWAT team for wildlife. It was officially launched in March 2001, and is jointly managed by the government and WildAid.

"When I came to Cambodia, everyone was talking about conservation, but nobody was doing anything about it," says the feisty woman whose passion for saving wildlife at any cost has become almost legendary. "This is the only dedicated task force fighting the wildlife trade in the whole of Asia. And it's working."

By any standards, Gauntlett is an unlikely crusader. She has ruffled feathers at every level, and lambasted her way through insurmountable obstacles. Some even claim she has overstepped the boundaries of conservation with her hardball tactics of arresting small-time traders. But the bottom line is that the open sale of meat and live wild animals has been stopped in Phnom Penh and its surroundings. Gauntlett has occasionally received death threats, but even traders with high-level protection have been forced underground.

On one recent sting, the unit confiscated 220 macaques from a house on National Route 5. The consignment was destined for the Vietnamese border, where it would probably have been divided into smaller lots and smuggled over on motorcycles or ox carts—part of a long-established route that continues to flourish. On another occasion, a truck loaded with 2.8 tons of wildlife specimens and illegal forest products was stopped on the outskirts of Phnom Penh. "You have to start with enforcement," says Gauntlett, who also advocates community-based programs to provide an alternative source of income for poachers. "Without that, it's a free-for-all."

Her words are almost prophetic. Hours later an informer phones with details of a pick-up truck filled with protected wildlife heading towards the town of Kompong Cham. Immediately, a team from the mobile patrol unit is dispatched to set up a roadblock. The truck is identified by its license plate and pulled over. Inside police find twenty-four live pangolins, five cobras, eight soft-shell turtles, and a cage full of doves.

The pangolins, snakes, and turtles are transported to a nearby national park and released. The birds end up being taken to Phnom Tamao. And the driver receives an important lesson, which Gauntlett hopes will reverberate higher up the chain. Trafficking wildlife is illegal and those who take the risk must be ready to pay the penalty—although the reality in Cambodia is that those in power rarely get touched. 🐦

RIGHT
**Bokor National Park**

*Cambodian National Forestry Rangers release a couple of Slow Loris' back into their natural habitat. Loris' are popular pets in SE Asia and demand for these docile creatures remains strong.*

LEFT
**Bokor National Park**

*The rescued Slow-Loris awakes, ready to be released into the wild.*

"This is the only dedicated task force fighting the wildlife trade in the whole of Asia. And it's working."

# SAVING ASIA'S LAST FRONTIERS

**It takes three weeks of trekking over icy mountain passes and across fast-flowing streams and rivers to reach the village of Tahundan in the north of Burma. The village is made up of a collection of huts plus a small monastery perched on a hilltop. Beyond is a jumble of towering peaks and snow-capped mountains so spectacular that it dazzles even the most hardened traveler.**

In early 1997, the inhabitants of this remote village awoke to an extraordinary sight. A group of exhausted men was emerging from a clearing in the forest after a three-week expedition from the town of Putao. Among them was the first white man they had seen in decades. That man was Alan Rabinowitz and what he brought promised to change their world forever.

Rabinowitz's mission was ambitious: to survey this unexplored wilderness near the India-China border as part of a government plan to turn it into Burma's largest national park. For the veteran biologist, the repercussions went far beyond compiling lists of animal species and types of vegetation. If the project received the go-ahead, it could help preserve one of the country's last unbroken forest areas from the ravages of loggers and poachers. "Burma still has the largest standing areas of forest in the Indo-Pacific region relative to its size," says Rabinowitz, an American who is widely recognized as one of the great pioneers of conservation in remote corners of the globe. "Many of the big species are already hunted out. But if you keep the forests, the populations can bounce back."

It took another eighteen months of long drawn-out discussions and deeply frustrating setbacks before Rabinowitz's grand vision became a reality. On 12 November 1998, however, Mount Hkakabo Razi was officially declared a national park. Now Rabinowitz and his team from the New York-based Wildlife Conservation Society are busily surveying other biological hot spots in a bid to safeguard what is left of the region's increasingly empty forests.

In a world where high-profile wildlife busts typically grab the headlines, scientific expeditions such as this often go unnoticed. But identifying core areas of intact forest with high species potential is a vital and necessary first step towards restoring wildlife populations. Without that every other weapon in the conservation armory is irrelevant. "The key is to find those areas of high biodiversity and then to protect them," said the outspoken New Yorker. "In the short term, you have to save animal species and habitat. If you wait too long, there will be nothing left to save."

"Increased cross border cooperation and more involvement of police agencies in fighting nature crime is essential if Asia is to maintain its beautiful wildlife, rich protected areas, and important watersheds."

—Senator Kraisak Choonhavan, President of WildAid Foundation Thailand

The month-long expedition to the Mount Hkakabo area, jointly undertaken with the University of Yangon, had other consequences. One day, Rabinowitz met a poor hunter coming in from the forest carrying a deer-like creature in his basket. The animal, which had small hooves and black legs, turned out to be the black barking deer, or muntjac, whose only other known population was more than 1,600 kilometers away in southwest China. On another occasion, Rabinowitz identified a wholly new species of leaf deer, known to the locals as the *pe gyi*.

Not one to rest on his laurels, Rabinowitz's next proposal to the government was even more far-reaching: to create a giant tiger reserve connecting Mount Hkakabo and the northern forest complex with the Hukaung Valley, a spectacularly beautiful region protected by the great floodwaters of the Himalayas. The protected area would cover at least 20,000 square kilometers of evergreen forest and grasslands, making it the largest tiger reserve in the world—as well as critical habitat for Asian elephants, clouded leopards, and other rare mammals.

In late 2002, a team of WCS researchers led by Tony Lynam, a young Australian biologist, spent two and a half months surveying the most promising jungle sites in the Hukaung Valley. Relying on maps dating back to the 1940s, when this region was used by Americans to construct the infamous Ledo Road, they conducted almost 1,000 interviews with forest people. They also collected some 4,000 photographs from special infrared cameras strapped to trees. The findings indicated that there could be as many as sixty tigers in this remote valley, representing perhaps the largest viable population of tigers in Burma.

The best news came fifteen months later, in March 2004, when the government gave the final go-ahead for the proposed tiger reserve. For Rabinowitz this was the final proof that the Burmese authorities were serious about conservation. If all goes according to plan, he believes that the region could one day become a center for ecotourism, an industry that would help to reduce the incentive for poaching and bring additional income to the local people.

The creation of a protected area connecting far-flung populations of tigers is an example of the new dynamism shaking up the fuddy-duddy conservation world, raising hopes that the recent sharp decline of some of Asia's most endangered species can be halted, if not reversed. The question now for conservationists like Lynam is how fast it can be achieved. Every year, after the monsoon rains have ended, dozens of Lisu hunters migrate to the Hukaung valley from the mountains to the north. Armed with poison darts and snares, they crisscross this "lost" valley for months at a time in search of wild animals to sell or barter in the far-off market towns. "This is critical habitat. And it's disappearing," says Lynam. "This is the one chance we have of safeguarding it."

The setting up of national parks in Burma, however, raises a host of other sensitive issues that go far beyond the protection of wildlife. International environmental organizations must now decide whether they are willing to work hand-in-hand with regimes that have appalling human rights records and are subject to boycotts. These organizations must also consider whether the fate of animals is to be viewed as more important than the fate of local peoples. Rabinowitz, for his part, has no doubt about the rights of what he is doing. "Policies and regimes come and go, but conservation is forever," he says. "My task is simple. I will do whatever it takes to save wildlife." 🐦

**Hukaung Valley
Myanmar, 2004**

*The recently declared
8,400 square mile
Hukaung Valley tiger
reserve in northern
Myanmar is the largest
protected area for big
cats on earth.*

# The Conservationist

*Seub Nakhasathien*

The photograph is old and faded. It shows a man with thick rimmed glasses clutching a slow loris in the darkness and pulling the creature to safety. The image was taken more than 15 years ago in Thailand's remote Western forest complex. It is typical of many photographs that have survived of Seub Nakhasathien, a man who tirelessly campaigned to save the country's wild animals and forests.

Seub took his own life on a cool morning in September 1990 when the burden of living became too much to bear. Not long before, he had told a colleague. "If one more has to die in Huay Kha Khaeng, that must be me." Tragically, through death, he probably achieved more than in life.

Born to a small farmer's family in Prachin Buri, Seub grew up with a passion for nature. After graduating from university, he joined the Royal Forestry Department. He was to remain a civil servant for the remainder of his days.

Seub's uncompromising dedication and honesty put him at odds with those in positions of power. He saw himself as a representative of the animals whose job it was to protect the wildlife and forests. But he found himself battling against a system that was stacked against him.

When Seub complained about logging concessions that were awarded within the sanctuary, his protests were met with silence. When he drew the attention of his superiors to groups of influential hunting parties operating within the park, he was instructed to work harder. Even his requests for more rangers were ignored. In the end, he had nowhere to turn.

Seub's memory lives on in a foundation that has been set up to continue his life's work. The Seub Nakhasathien Foundation provides funds to support the rangers and villagers who live around the two wildlife sanctuaries, which were once his home. It also campaigns on broader environmental issues such as the building of roads through national parks and the construction of hydroelectric dams that threaten the surrounding watersheds.

There have been other changes too. A barbed wire fence extending for 117 km around Huay Kha Khaeng has been erected to help forestry staff to guard the sanctuary. Now there are plans to extend the fence along the remaining stretch of the wildlife reserve.

Not far from where Seub worked, a memorial has been built in his honour. It comprises his former home, a commemorative statue and a visitors' centre that hosts special educational events. Princess Maha Chakri Srindhorn, a member of the revered Thai Royal family, inaugurated the complex in April 1993–evidence of the new groundswell of support for conservation within the kingdom. Outside the simple collection of buildings, sambar and barking deer graze the park lands, the most visible of the 600 odd species of birds, mammals and reptiles that inhabit the sanctuary.

Some eighteen months after his death, an even more significant event occurred. Huay Kha Khaeng and neighboring Thung Yai Naresuan were declared a UNESCO World Heritage Site. The new status came in recognition of their unique diversity of animals and plants. Seub had long championed that cause in the face of official opposition. It is proof that his ultimate sacrifice was not in vain.

# CELEBRITY POWER

Luk Gaed, one of Thailand's top models, is seated under a gigantic silver-covered umbrella opposite a bank of spotlights in the Thai capital, Bangkok. It's 1:00 p.m. on a Thursday in early March 2003 and the final touches have already been made to the set. Adjusting the microphone, Luk visibly relaxes, looks straight ahead and begins. The lights are on. The cameras are rolling. "While tigers are being hunted, other wild cats like leopards and clouded leopards are also being killed," says the thirty-two-year-old former beauty queen who grew up in New York City. "Why let this or any beautiful creature become an ornament for somebody else?"

Luk Gaed is just one of a half-dozen or so local celebrities taking part in a high profile television advertising campaign called the Asian Conservation Awareness Program (ACAP) organized by WildAid. The scenes accompanying the ones filmed in the studio are intentionally graphic. A giant sea turtle lies upside down as poachers rip open its belly with a bloody machete; a full-grown Asiatic black bear falls from a tree, shot for its paws and its gall bladder; an elephant with enormous, gleaming white tusks is attacked by a gang of poachers, who will sell the ivory on the world's black markets.

It's a far cry from the soft approach taken by many conservation organizations in recent years. But like the successful advertising campaigns that shamed Western buyers out of fur coats back in the 1970s, it has one overriding aim: to shatter the complacency of the general public about the plight of some of the world's most endangered species. To do so, it uses some of Asia's best-known celebrities as role models and presenters.

Jackie Chan first stepped into this campaigning work in early 1997. The star of movies such as *Shanghai Nights* and *Rush Hour* was working on location in Sun City, South Africa. Approached by Rebecca Chen and Peter Knights of the Global Survival Network, he was shown a film about the slaughter of elephants, rhinos, and other endangered species. Chan remembers that day only too well. "After I saw the video, I had tears in my eyes," he says. " I saw the people killing tigers, elephants, turtles, and bears and I said, 'Yes, I've got to do this.' "

Over the next two years, up to 50 million viewers in Asia saw the region's most famous movie star and producer calling for an end to the slaughter and trade in wild animals. Chan's image was beamed into Taiwan and Hong Kong and even into China. Gone was the easy-going comic persona

## Hong Kong, China

*Michelle Yeoh poses with Hope, one of two South China tigers on their way to South Africa at Hong Kong's Chep Lap Kok Airport. Pacific Airways helped transport two Chinese tigers from Beijing to South Africa as part of the Save China's Tigers project, pioneered by the Save China's Tiger Foundation.*

with the memorable stunts and the bulging triceps. This time the message was for real. "If we can stop people buying endangered-species products and find the funds to support conservation projects, we can save these animals so that they will continue to survive in their natural habitat," he says.

When asked why it should bother a high-flying multimillionaire, Hong Kong film star if some of the world's most endangered species are wiped off the planet, Chan's answer takes on a more serious tone. "If our descendents have to ask us why they can only see animals like rhinoceroses in paintings and photographs, how can we tell them that it's because some people among our ancestors felt that rhinoceros horns had medicinal value and killed them; and that shawls and scarves made from *shahtoosh*, the wool of the Tibetan antelope, were exquisite and expensive—and therefore killed them as well?" he says.

Other film stars, politicians, singers, and actors have added their voices to the growing chorus attempting to raise awareness about environmental issues. Former "Bond girl" Michelle Yeoh threw her weight behind the campaign. So did Asian heartthrob Tony Leung and respected former Thai Prime Minister Anand Panyarachun. The latest addition to the ranks of wildlife campaigners is Hollywood actress Angelina Jolie, who announced she would invest up to US $5 million in a new reserve in a former Khmer Rouge stronghold in western Cambodia.

The celebrity-led campaigns are already having an impact. In Taiwan, more than three-quarters of the people who viewed the ACAP television advertisements said they would never buy products linked to endangered species again. Meanwhile in China, the unthinkable is happening. In some major cities, consumers have actually begun to turn away from purchases of certain protected birds and animals. The change is due to the increasing awareness that the trade is illegal and to the fear of disease following the outbreak of SARS.

It is in Asia's schools, however, that the battle will eventually be lost or won. On a starry evening in March, Dr. Bibhab Kumar Talukdar lectures a group of students on the need for action. Bibhab heads up Aaranyak Assam, conservation organization based in Northeast India. His operation is small, with only limited resources, but it is making a difference. After showing slides of some of the most threatened species in India, Bibhab launches into a diatribe about why these animals must be saved. "We conservationists have failed," he says. "We have failed because hunting and poaching continue despite all our efforts."

For Bibhab, one way of combating the dangerously high level of apathy has been to bring older children from the nearby cities to spend time in the national parks. It's an opportunity for the students to learn about the wonders of the great one-horned Indian rhinoceros as well as the fish-eating eagle and other rare but endemic species of birds. The approach is effective not only because it educates a younger generation, but because sons and daughters return home and lecture their parents on the need to safeguard wild animals for the future. The hope is that these young men and women will grow up viewing the consumption of endangered wildlife with the same disdain that they now regard cannibalism. Eventually, some of them may even reach positions of power where they can directly influence protection of the environment.

It's a long shot by any stretch of the imagination. But for people like Bibhab and Chan, raising public awareness may be the best chance we have to save what is left of the natural world. Without activism, education, and enforcement, there will be nothing but a slow and irreversible decline. "It's very simple," says Chan during a rare interlude in his busy work schedule. "Do not buy any products made from endangered animals."

*School children study a large billboard outside a local school in Phnom Penh. Part of a government education program aimed at creating a national awareness of Cambodia's wildlife laws.*

"Many endangered animals become extinct only to satisfy the vanity of humans. We must ask from our hearts: are humans such a selfish and ignorant species?"

—Jackie Chan

Jackie Chan, an internationally recognized film star and martial arts expert, has been a long time advocate of animal rights. As a leading international spokesperson for Active Conservation Awareness Program (ACAP), Chan has frequently spoken out against the trafficking of endangered animals worldwide. One of the first Asian actors to call for fair treatment , purchasing alternatives and public awareness of the atrocities committed against the many endangered species currently in demand, he has since been joined by countless other media celebrities, as well as religious figures from all over the world.

# IS EXTINCTION REALLY FOREVER?

In a tall glass cylindrical jar kept under lock and key in the basement of the Australian Museum in Sydney sits the anemic looking but perfectly preserved body of a Tasmanian tiger. Valued at US $1.1 million for insurance purposes, it is the only one of its kind, with all others believed to have been killed by early settlers or farmers. The last known Tasmanian tiger, or thylacine, died in captivity in Hobart Zoo on 7 September 1936. Precisely half a century later, this carnivorous marsupial with the distinctive stripes on its back and hindquarters was officially declared extinct.

If a team of Australian scientists have their way, however, the Tasmanian tiger could quite literally be brought back to life. The man behind this extraordinarily ambitious—and some believe impossible project—is a zoologist and former scholar of paleontological research by the name of Professor Mike Archer. Inspired by the successful cloning of Dolly the sheep, which was hailed as one of the most significant breakthroughs of the twentieth century, Archer began to look into the prospect of re-creating the Tasmanian tiger using similar technology. His work received the full support of the Australian Museum.

Learning that a female tiger pup had been preserved in alcohol in the museum vaults for more than 100 years, Archer set about trying to extract the DNA necessary to map the genes of this wolf-like creature. The initial breakthrough came in April 2000, when scientists from the evolutionary biology unit successfully removed small samples of heart, liver, muscle, and bone tissue from the preserved female tiger fetus. Two years later, more DNA was extracted from two other preserved pups. The extractions formed the first step in what Archer believes could lead to the first-ever reversal of extinction. "We were told by so many people in the scientific community that it was near to impossible to clone an extinct species," says Professor Archer, former director of the Australian Museum, now dean of the Faculty of Science at the University of New South Wales. "But now the dream is starting to become a reality."

Removing the internal organs, however, was the easy part of this experiment. Now, Dr. Don Colgan, head of the Australian Museum's Evolutionary Biology Unit, and his team are attempting to make large quantity copies of all the animal's genes so that they can be used to construct synthetic chromosomes. If all goes according to plan, they eventually hope to insert Tasmanian tiger genetic

Species that have become locally extinct in Vietnam include the Sumatran rhino, the kouprey, the Siamese crocodile and the Eld's deer.

material into the host cell of a near relative such as the Tasmanian Devil, which could act as a surrogate mother.

"This project is like a 17-million-piece jigsaw puzzle," says Dr. Colgan, who will continue to oversee the project in collaboration with Archer. "If it is possible to obtain enough viable DNA, then cloning could provide a possible option."

Although the final outcome of the project is far from certain, the $56-million US experiment has raised hopes that the Australian team may eventually be able to restore to life a species that took more than 50 million years to evolve. If that happens, it would be one of the most revolutionary breakthroughs in scientific history. It could also have enormous repercussions for the future survival of some of the world's most endangered wildlife species.

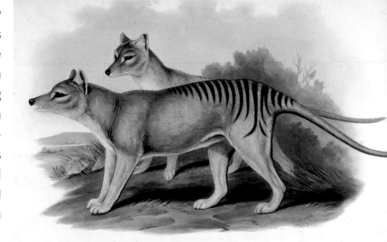

Not surprisingly, the work carried out by Professor Archer and his colleagues has proved as controversial as it has been ground breaking. Since he first launched his scientific odyssey, Archer has been accused of everything, from playing God to squandering money that would be better spent on conservation of existing animals and wildlife habitat. But the fifty-eight-year-old Princeton University graduate makes few apologies. "It sets out to redress our immoral actions when we willfully and wrongfully exterminated the animal," he says. "It's an opportunity to question whether extinction really is forever."

*Early illustration of the Thylacine, now extinct.*

Bringing a lost species like the Tasmanian tiger back to life is only one of the many uses of cloning, which is fast rolling back the frontiers of science and technology, and throwing up a host of moral and ethical questions that have yet to be fully resolved.

In an even bigger feat of pioneering, researchers at Advanced Cell Technology in Massachusetts announced in early 2001 that they had successful cloned the first ever endangered species, a type of rare ox known as the gaur. Although the baby gaur died within forty-eight hours of being born, thanks to a common case of dysentery, scientists soon turned their attention to cloning another endangered species: the banteng, a type of wild cow hunted for its slender curved horns. The first banteng clone was born to an Angus cow on April Fools Day in 2003.

Even among wildlife conservationists the value of cloning technology is under debate.

No one can predict the extent to which it might really help safeguard Asia's wildlife or whether it will ultimately mass-produce animals that will end up as scientific curiosities or prized items in a private collection. Some of the most vocal critics argue that the money would be better spent on protecting existing wildlife and habitat rather than producing *Jurassic Park*-like species that may lack the necessary prey and prove unsuitable for release in the wild. Legendary British naturalist David Attenborough has few illusions about what the experiment really means for conservation. "Bringing the Tasmanian tiger back to life won't restore the environment," he says. "If it happens, the animals will end up in a zoo."

Yet, in the increasingly heated debate, there is another equally terrifying reality. Failure to clone or farm extremely rare animals could well lead to their extinction. Although few people want to see tiger farms, bear farms, or panda clones, when all other conservation measures have been tried and failed that has to be a final option. Unless cloning comes to the rescue, some of Asia's rarest animals may vanish forever. ▲

*The only preserved specimen remaining of a Thylacine pup, kept in a vault at the Australian Museum in Sydney.*

# BACK FROM THE BRINK?

**Jane Goodall, who has spent more than forty years of her life studying chimpanzees, has a list of rare animal species that she likes to read to audiences on her international lecture tours. The list includes animals such as the Californian condor, the whooping crane, and the black robin. The species are totally different, but they have one thing in common. They all bounced back from the brink of extinction.**

"The story that I like best is the one about the black robin," says Goodall, who now acts as a roving ambassador, preaching the value of conservation to people of all backgrounds, creeds, and colors. "In the early 1980s, there were only two breeding pairs restricted to one island in the Pacific. Today there are forty breeding pairs and numbers are on the increase."

More than just the black robin, the whooping crane, or the chimpanzee, Goodall is fighting for all wild species when she tours the world opening people's eyes to the environmental destruction taking place around them. It's her conviction that individuals can and will make a difference that provides a glimmer of hope for some of Asia's most endangered wildlife.

"You have to be positive," she says with a quiet resolution that belies her seventy years of age. "People have the power to change the world. Habitats that have been destroyed can be rescued. Culture can be changed. Everyone can contribute a little something whether by donating money or by giving up some of their time to support conservation work."

In the battle to save Asia's dwindling wildlife populations, raising public awareness about the plight of nature, pressuring governments to take action, and penalizing companies or countries with poor environmental records are all vital steps that must be taken. But the most critical of all is to identify and save the last remaining centers of biodiversity while they still exist. It's something akin to guarding Noah's Ark. Animals are finite. Once the last Javanese rhino or snow leopard is gone, it will be too late, barring unproven acts of scientific wizardry to bring them back.

Indeed the real issues are these: how badly do we want to preserve the world's most endangered species, and at what cost are we prepared to do so? According to the influential Washington-based Conservation International, it would cost US $23 billion per year for the next ten years to create and effectively police the number of protected areas necessary to maintain current wildlife populations around the world. That may sound like a lot, but it is less than half what America spends each year on soft drinks. Or seen another way, it is around 2 percent of what governments

> "People have the power to change the world. Habitats that have been destroyed can be rescued. Culture can be changed. Everyone can contribute a little something whether by donating money or by giving up some of their time to support conservation work."

spend annually on supporting agricultural production, energy use, road transportation and commercial fisheries.

Aaron Bruner, who works at Conservation International's Center for Applied Biodiversity Science, has little doubt about the long-term value of such an investment. "Protected areas are the cornerstone of conservation efforts worldwide," he says. "Areas of irreplaceable biological importance will be lost if we do not act soon."

Realistically, however, it's going to take a lot more than money to solve the problems of illegal logging, deforestation, and the plunder of the wild. Billions of dollars are spent every year on the war against drugs. Yet the trafficking of cocaine or heroin remains at horrifying levels and drug addiction is present in every society. The reason is simple. Enforcement alone does not address the root causes such as poverty, social injustice, and ignorance.

Many Asian people eat wildlife because they have done so for generations and because they do not know it is wrong. But habits change and cultures evolve. Even in the most remote areas of China, Western medicine is making inroads, banishing the bizarre superstitions that spur much of the consumption of animal parts. Children are growing up with a new understanding of the value of nature thanks to programs funded by local and international conservation organizations and governments. Take the process one step further and there is a glimmer of hope. If there were no buyers of ivory, tiger skins, or rhino horns, poachers would no longer find it profitable to kill these animals.

"Education, education, education," says Andy Fisher, head of the wildlife crimes unit at Britain's Metropolitan Police. "People must realize that if they buy an endangered animal, they are contributing to its extinction."

Fortunately, despite Asia's rapidly growing population and dwindling resources, there are many organizations and individuals helping to address the crisis. Vo Quay, the man fondly referred to as the "father of conservation" in Vietnam, is racing against time to confront these gargantuan issues. He knows that the solution to the wildlife problem is as much a question of improving the lot of villagers, as it is direct enforcement and less corrupt government. And he is doing what he can, given the country's limited funds, to tackle problems head on. "We try to educate the people at every level and to reduce the poverty of people living near the forests," he says. "But it will take at least five or ten years to achieve this goal."

The people of Pangasinan, a small, central Philippine province, tell a simple story. Each generation, they say merely borrows the world's forests and myriad birds and animals. It is the duty of every man and woman to pass on this precious legacy to their children in the same state that they receive it.

"Protected areas are the cornerstone of conservation efforts worldwide," says Bruner. "Areas of irreplaceable biological importance will be lost if we do not act soon."

But in a world already stripped of much of its forests and wildlife by greed and over-consumption, such ancient wisdom is insufficient to solve the deep-seated problems. "We need to do more than act as custodians," says Goodall. "We desperately need to save what is left of the natural world and to heal the wounds. We must do it for our children."

And that's the bottom line. The potential to solve the current crisis is now in our hands. There are realistic and achievable solutions, but we must act. If we don't, future generations will inherit a world without forests and wildlife, a world subject to untold natural calamities. Time is running out. 🐃

**Saravane, Laos**
**1911**

*Hunting Expedition*

# ACKNOWLEDGEMENTS

I am grateful to the following people for directly or indirectly assisting me in writing this book. Their names are printed here in no particular order. Vu Ngoc Thanh, Carolyn Jensen Chadwick, Jill Robinson, Dr Barbara Maas, Ashok Kumar, Mike Pandey, Vivek Menon, Dipankar Ghose, Belinda Wright, Firip Blenkinsop (thanks for Mongla), Hoang Quoc Dung, Trinh Le Nguyen, Dr Bibhab Kumar Talukdar, Pradeep Nath, Sawaek Pinsinchai, Aroon Promphan, Sompoad Srikosamatara, Thanit Palasuwan, Pornpen Payakkaporn, Prasert Sri Yongtong, Sir David Attenborough, Jane Goodall, Mary Lewis, Jackie Chan, Solon So, Prawing Klinkai, Dr Antony Lynam, Edwin Wiek, Paul Hilton, Colin Poole, Rita Lam, John Goodrich, Endi Zhang, Olie Pin-Fat, Dr Ullas Karanth, Vo Quay, Nguyen Dao Ngoc Van, Douglas Hendrie, Julia Shaw, Professor Pham Duc Duong, Stuart Issett, Michiko, George Schaller, John Thomas, Jake Brunner, Aaron Bruner, David Mead, Anthony Simms, Helen Leavesley, Samuel James Taylor, Sun Hean, Chey Yuthearith, Hong Daravuth, Mark Bowman, Timothy Redford, Suwanna Gauntlett, Brian Kennerley, Nick Marx, Michael Hayes, Rebecca Weldon, Jean Dauplay, Hunter Weiler, Eva Galabru, Kathleen Hayes, Krissana Kaewplang, Andrew Marshall, Guy Marris, Dr Don Colgan, Rajesh Ghimire, Bruce Kekule, Kiran Man Chitrakar, James Compton, Chris Shepherd, Hardi Baktiantoro, Rosek Nursahid, Francis Middlehurst, Ian Singleton, M Pasha, U Tin Than, Sergei Bereznuk, Derek Welton, Bob Martin, Andy Fisher, Bill Jordan, Debbie Banks, Faith Doherty, Charles Mackay, Dominique Roland, Anhar Lupiz, Dr Robert Mather, Bill Young and Dr Lo Yan-wo.

Several people asked to remain anonymous. To these individuals and to the countless others who helped me in some way, please accept my enormous debt of gratitude. Without your kindness and wisdom, this book would not be.

Finally, I would like to offer special thanks to the following: publisher Raoul Goff together with Robbie Schmidt, Noah Potkin, Lisa Fitzpatrick and the team at Palace Press for their vision and support; book producer Adam Oswell for coming up with the idea for the project and then giving me the opportunity to work on it; Jim Pollard for patiently reading through all my drafts and assisting with research; Patrick Brown for his hard work with the photography; Nic Dunlop for his insight, his enthusiasm and his unwavering sense of justice; Mangal Man Shakya and Mrigen Barua for providing assistance well beyond the call of duty; Steve Galster for believing in the project when others lost faith; Roland Neveu for his photo-editing skills and immense experience; my wife Cristina for wading through the mountains of manuscripts, putting up with my long absences and providing a never ending source of encouragement; and finally my daughter Carla. This book is also for you so that you may grow up in a world where there are still wild animals.

—Ben Davies

Note about Names:

The names of some people referred to in the book have been changed to protect their identities.

Any similarity to people of the same name is purely coincidental.

# Sources

## Books

Askins, Charles. *Asian Jungle-African Bush*. 1959. Telegraph Press. Harrisburg.

Beard, Peter. *The End of the Game*. 1963. Chronicle Books. San Francisco.

Chadwick, Douglas. *The Fate of the Elephant*. 1992. Sierra Club Books. San Francisco.

Chou, Ta-Kuan. *Customs of Cambodia*. 1987. The Siam Society. Bangkok.

Day, Michael. *Fight for the Tiger*. 1995. Headline Book Publishing. London.

Douglas-Hamilton, Ian and Oria. *Battle for the Elephants*. 1992. Penguin Books USA. New York.

Fitzgerald, Sarah. *International Wildlife Trade: Whose Business Is It?* 1989. World Wildlife Fund. Baltimore.

Gillson, Lindsey. *Tigers*. 1997. Care for the Wild International. Horsham.

Green, Alan. *Animal Underworld*. 1999. Public Affairs. New York.

Grove, Richard. *Nature and the Orient*. 1998. Oxford University Press. Oxford.

Hemley, Ginette. *International Wildlife Trade. A CITES Sourcebook*. 1994. World Wildlife Fund.

Hoser, Raymond. *Smuggled. The Underground Trade in Australia's Wildlife*. 1993. Kotabi Publishing. Victoria.

Hutton, Jon. *Endangered Species, Threatened Convention*. 2000. Earthscan Publications. London.

Kiernan, Ben. *The Pol Pot Regime: Race, Power and Genocide in Cambodia*. 1996. Yale University Press.

Leakey, Richard. *The Sixth Extinction*. 1995. Doubleday. New York.

Lintner, Bertil. *Blood Brothers: Crime, Business and Politics in Asia*. 2002. Silkworm Books. Chiang Mai.

Menon, Vivek. *Tusker. The Story of the Asian Elephant*. 2002. Penguin Books India. New Delhi.

Nooren, Hanneke and Claridge, Gordon. *Wildlife Trade in Laos: the End of the Game*. 2001. IUCN. Amsterdam.

Rabinowitz, Alan. *Beyond the Last Village*. 2001. Island Press. Washington.

Smythies. E. A. *Big Game Shooting in Nepal*. 1942. Thacker, Spink & Co. Calcutta.

Thapar, Valmik. *Saving Wild Tigers*. 2001. Permanent Black. Delhi.

Wilson, Edward. *The Diversity of Life*. 1992. Penguin Books. London.

Wood, Alexander. *The Root Causes of Biodiversity Loss*. 2000. Earthscan Publications. London.

## Reports

A Tale of Two Cities: A Comparative Study of Chinese Medicine Markets in San Francisco and New York City. L.A. Henry, TRAFFIC North America. 2004 World Wildlife Fund.

A God in Distress: Threat of Poaching and the Ivory Trade. Vivek Menon, Raman Sukumar and Ashok Kumar. Wildlife Protection Society of India.

Back in Business: Elephant Poaching and the Ivory Black Markets of Asia. 2002. Environmental Investigation Agency.

Borderline. An Assessment of Wildlife Trade in Vietnam. James Compton. 1998. World Wildlife Fund.

CITES and the Wildlife Trade in Nepal. 2001. Mangal Man Shakya.

Conflict of Interest: The Uncertain Future of Burma's Forests. 2003. Global Witness.

Crime Against Nature – Organized Crime and the Illegal Wildlife Trade. The Endangered Species Project.

End of the Line. The Global Threat to Sharks. 2001. WildAid.

Examination of the Vietnamese Wildlife Trade. 1997. Emma Woodford.

Far From A Cure - The Tiger Trade Revisited. Kristin Nowell. 1999. Traffic International.

Flying Without Wings. Investigation on Parrot Trade in Indonesia. 2002. Profauna Indonesia.

How Much will Effective Protected Area Systems Cost? Aaron Bruner, John Hanks and Lee Hannah. 2003. Conservation International.

Hunting and Wildlife Trade in Tropical and Sub-Tropical Asia. Compiled by Elizabeth Bennett. 2002. Wildlife Conservation Society.

International Wildlife Trade and Organized Crime. Dee Cook, Martin Roberts and Jason Lowther. 2002. Traffic

Killed for a Cure. Judy Mills and Peter Jackson. Traffic International.

Legal Eagle. RSPB Investigations Newsletter. April 2002.

On the Trail of New Species. George Schaller. August 1998. National Wildlife Federation.

Lethal Experiment. How the CITES-Approved Ivory Sale Led to Increased Elephant Poaching. Environmental Investigation Agency.

Prepared and Shipped. A Review of the Effects of Capture, Handling and Transport. 2000. Dr Barbara Maas.

Primate Meat Trade in Sumatra, Indonesia. 2002. Profauna Indonesia.

Resources, Conflict and Corruption. 2003. Global Witness.

Rhino Translocation. 1999. Nepal Forum of Environmental Journalists.

South and South East Asian Ivory Market. 2001. Esmond Martin and Daniel Stiles.

Switching Channels: Wildlife Trade Routes into Europe and the UK. 2002. WWF/ Traffic.

Thailand's Tiger Economy. Debbie Banks and Faith Doherty. 2002. Environmental Investigation Agency.

Trade of Elephants and Elephant Products in Myanmar. Chris Shepherd. 2002. Traffic Southeast Asia.

Traded Towards Extinction: The Role of the UK in Wildlife Trade. Trevor Lawson. 2002. World Wildlife Fund.

Wildlife Markets of Medan: Large and Largely Illegal. Chris Shepherd. 2000. Traffic Southeast Asia.

Wildlife Trade Research. 2,000. WildAid and David Shepherd Conservation Foundation.

Wrap Up the Trade. An International Campaign to Save the Endangered Tibetan Antelope. 2001. The International Fund for Animal Welfare.